LIFE THROUGH CRISIS

Returning to the Father

Tanisha Williams

Copyright ©
2022 Tanisha Williams
ISBN: 978-1-955579-06-3

Scripture quotations are taken from the New International Version, New Living Translation or New King James Version, copyright 1996, 2004, 2007 by Tyndale House Foundation. Used by permission of Tyndale House Publishers, Inc. Carol Stream, Illinois 60188. All Rights Reserved.

ALL RIGHTS RESERVED.

This book contains material protected under International and Federal Copyright Laws and Treaties. Any unauthorized reprint or use of this material is prohibited.

No part of this book may be reproduced or transmitted in any form or by any means, electronic or mechanical, including photocopying, recording, or by any information storage and retrieval system without express written permission of the publisher, except in the case of brief quotations embodied in critical reviews and certain non-commercial uses permitted by copyright law.

Publishing in the United States of America

Publisher: Luminous Publishing
www.luminouspublishing.com
For bulk orders or other inquiries, email:
info@luminouspublishing.com

"And the LORD shall guide thee continually, and satisfy thy soul in drought, and make fat thy bones: and thou shalt be like a watered garden, and like a spring of water, whose waters fail not." - Isaiah 58:11

Dedication

This book is dedicated to my Heavenly Father, who loved me when I didn't love myself, and through His love, I'm becoming who He has called me to be.

Foreword

Crisis: a word that has been saturated in the airways of our recent social climate so loosely. It has become common to associate light affliction with this term, leaving the depth of understanding the fullness of embodying such an experience fragmentary. Crisis is much more than mild uncomfort or unwanted pain. It is not simply an ache or an uncomfortable happenstance; and, though it is admissible to acknowledge any amount of pain that one experiences in life, the applied differentiation and specificity of the depth of a crisis is paramount, especially when your crisis is attached to a greater purpose. When one embraces the assigned tests and trials strategically orchestrated for them with grace, it often draws them closer to the Ultimate Creator, and in turn, closer to destiny. The aspiration of crisis through Christ is not for the intention of destroying the soldier. The projection of purposeful affliction is to propel one into a greater showcase of strength and valor, amassing the necessary tools to conquer the greatest of unexpected twists and turns of life, while developing the wisdom to stand in the place of an example for others who might encounter comparable calamities. This book is a true depiction of what it means to, not only encounter struggle, but to embrace it with the grace that Christ did as he encountered the complexities of life in His flesh. This book illustrates the life of a soldier, who has taken numerous blows, many unexpected, but found a way to soar to a purpose-filled life in Christ. I admonish you to take the journey with the author and soldier to understand the cause, embodiment, and remedy for crisis.

Terell L. Williams,
CEO of Rich Fingers Brand

Prayer

As I embark on this mission of writing a book, through Your guidance, I ask that You project Your Spirit in a way that takes me out of the equation. Though I know that this is my story, it is You who is being glorified through the production of this book. For every tear I have shed, to the burdens I have left at Your altar, I want this to reflect the humility of a once broken woman coming to the knowledge of her worth through the Being that created her. Let this be a reminder that "all things are possible" because Your Word declares so. Lord, I pray for every person who will encounter the words written about my journey. I pray that someone will read this journey and become compelled to start their own journey with You because of the topics discussed; and, as they experience it, I want it to be known that the glory belongs to You and You alone. We all have been giving this walk called Life. Some of us have travelled a much deeper and darker road that has eventually led us to You.

Many have grown up in the church and need a refresher to remember all the promises that You granted us through Your Word. Whatever path it might be, Father, I pray for the words in this print to echo out Your Love. The pages of this book reveal my strengths and weaknesses. It required much courage to write about my experiences as one of Your children. Being set apart has its pains; but, with it, there is an unspeakable joy that can't be given by the world. Thank You for the privilege of being able to write the testimony You have given me. I know that I have not always lived up to Your expectations of me, but I want my readers to know that by ultimately submitting to Your will, with Your Grace and Mercy, one could accomplish more than they ever imagined. To know that You are not looking for perfection, rather one whose heart is willing to surrender to Your guidance of transformation, ushered peace and serenity. The sufferings that have come to make this possible will not stop the glory of who You are in my life. You are my anchor of hope, and anyone who reads this will know that it is through Your Spirit that something so sacred can be produced. My hope is that readers will laugh, cry, and be in awe of my story. I want this caption of my life to inspire some readers to reach back out to You in submission and others to deepen their understanding of You. Take this writing, Lord, and do as You please. Allow the Holy Spirit to manifest through it, and, at the end of this, cause readers to give their hearts completely over to You. May their trust be strengthened, and restoration begin. I Love You, Jesus, and I'm so thankful to be called one of Your own. In Jesus' Name, Amen.

Table of Contents

Prologue 1
The Miracle of 93' 4
Battle Scars 14
Prayer 19
Rated PMG (Toxic) 20
Poem: Words I can't express 35
The Storm 39
You lived Where? 45
The System is Rigged! 56
Unforeseen 72
Girls Gone Wild! 78
Series of Unfortunate Events 85
Thank God for Jesus! 92
Poem: The mask has to come off. 97
Mr. Right? 107
Poem: You are Worth the Wait 126
What lesson did I learn from crossing paths with Randy? 131
The Prodigal's Daughter ✔ 136
Here we go again! 151
4-007 163
Big Easy 171
Phew! 177

Prologue

1 Peter 2:9 states, "But ye are a chosen generation, a royal priesthood, a holy nation, a peculiar people: that ye should shew forth the praises of him who hath called you out of darkness into His marvelous light." I remember the moment God broke the walls of my heart down and led me to His loving arms of freedom. I was roughly 16 or 17 years old. Though I'm not too sure of which age at the time, what truly mattered was that I had just opened my heart to a God that I had never seen or understood. In my years of living, although I didn't have a personal relationship with Jesus, it was the inkling in my spirit concerning what was right and wrong that made me believe this decision would change my reality. It wasn't until years later when I recognized that I was being placed in the center of God's will through Christ Himself despite the presence of my circumstances. Facing a detriment of feeling like life couldn't possibly become worse, I neglected my opportunity to truly be transformed by Christ. Eventually, I became aware that instead of mirroring His reflection, my life became a deadly cycle as I spiraled out of control before my true story written by God could be manifested as He interrupted the path I was on.

Delving deep into the past that a trailblazer would run from, transformation to the woman I am today wouldn't have been possible without fully acknowledging the missteps taken in my early adolescence and adulthood. I acknowledge that dismissing my feelings over the fact that life is not always sweet, would have probably put me in a better place in life; but, due to my young age and misguidance, I chased the wind of weed, pornography, and partying to ease the pain I felt inside. No one told me that God was the answer to life's troubles. I didn't grow up in a church or hear anyone introduce this God to me. In my perceived reality, I was alone.

Unbeknownst to me, God required a heart change and surrendering of my life completely: a process I wasn't ready to take on. I hoped that finding God on my own would give me some of the answers I was looking for. I had to be broken before the throne of the Creator. I didn't want to admit that my mental and emotional state of mind were at an all-time low. I began to search for answers at Perfecting Faith Church while living in Roosevelt, NY. I entered the church in a blind condition. As the singer sang and musicians played, I noticed that many around me apparently had a beautiful relationship with God. Instead of just flowing into the Spirit the same way they were, I could only think about overcoming pain and getting to know Christ for myself. I had no idea worship was the foundation to entering into the Lord's presence. It didn't register in my mind that God was so personable. Even when the message was delivered and the Pastor said to talk to God as the music played, I didn't know I could talk to Him at any given time.

While there, I met an amazing woman of God. She had a fire for Christ that I have never experienced before. Due to eventually leaving the church because I moved, I lost contact with her. Over the years, when a mini light captured me to journey back, I remembered the church and the woman. I prayed before going that God would reintroduce us. After three years, that moment happened. Though I had a great conversation with the women from the past, I walked out of that church empty physically; spiritually, I was ready for God to show me what church He truly wanted me to be a part of. I needed to find a place where God's Spirit dwelled, and I could get the revelation on how to connect with Christ. I wanted more because Christ was revealing Himself in ways I couldn't believe. I was in awe of God. Recalling the worship that was displayed at Perfecting Faith, I needed more. While I could have asked more questions about worship or Christ at that moment, it didn't deter me from chasing after the path I believed God was placing me on. Honestly, I was tired of the idols I placed before God. I learned the hard way that God removes our idols and allows them to make a fool out of us, not to bring harm, but for understanding that He is the only idol.

Although I couldn't see it, it would be the first step into becoming aware that this living God existed. We are to worship God in all areas of our lives. We have to be willing to allow God to reveal our hearts. I could have easily run like I did in the past, but thank God for Jesus; He wasn't through with me just yet. I no longer had to try and figure things out alone. If I chose to, it would have caused me to be prideful, discrediting God for bringing me out of the darkness and into His marvellous light. I'm thankful to Him that despite my sin, He didn't give up on me. While writing this, God has shown me that He was the answer, directing my life in a way that would please Him the most. Idolatry turns your heart into being wicked if the idol is not God. Learn this lesson that no one or thing can satisfy your life like the One who created you. I now have a new destination: Eternity in Heaven.

The Miracle of 93'

Before I fully get deeper into the day when my sinful life was interrupted by the Holy Spirit, I must start with my body being placed in my mother's womb by God. Every person put on the earth has a beginning that started from the moment of conception. The Bible says that before being developed in your mother's womb, God has already given you a life plan. I call it the blueprint to your choice destination. Jeremiah 1:5 states, *"Before I formed you in the womb, I knew you, before you were born, I set you apart; I appointed you as a prophet to the nations."* A prophet is known as someone who is an inspired teacher and proclaimer of the will of God. In order for such persons to fulfill this will upon the earth, we must first acknowledge and believe that God is real. One simply cannot follow a plan if you have no relationship or access to the one who has given it. This is where you choose the destiny requiring the relinquishing of your own works and the destiny designed from the one who created the entire world: a choice. Which will you decide?

"Now wait, Tanisha, you're saying we have a choice in our destination?" Absolutely! We have been given the free will to decide whether or not we shall follow the plan God has for us. In a world filled with enticing temptations; premarital sex, endless alcohol, and drugs that take you to "new heights," resisting the set foundation of the one who brought you forth for His purpose, can seem daunting. When a person has not grown up in the knowledge of Christ as Lord and Savior, the description above is pleasing to the eye. Yet, in His majesty and wisdom, He chooses to reveal Himself in a time where love meets the broken-hearted and offers redemption from the world's fantasy. Jesus, being the creator of all, foreknew the moment you would surrender your heart and seek Him for His will. You were planned from the beginning of time, even if, in societal terms, your parents conceived you unintentionally. He knows you better than you can know yourself; Jeremiah 1:5 is the foundation of that promise.

I recollect the sermon, **"When you don't understand what to do,"** preached by Bishop Noel Jones as a reference of acknowledgement that God formed us for His purpose. He didn't give credit to our biological parents, but the credit is given back to Him. If the credit is given to God, then the Scripture in Philippians 1:6, *"being confident of this, that He who began a good work in you will carry it on to completion until the day of Jesus Christ has to be finished,"* will manifest in your life accordingly. A friend of mine sent this sermon to me when I began writing this book. What she didn't know was that information from the Holy Spirit with this verse had already been given to me; hence, she provided confirmation of the direction I was being led in.

As the sermon continues, Bishop Noel discusses how Jeremiah believed that God deceived him because of the attacks he faced. This reminded me of the circumstances that led to my birth. You see, I felt like God didn't want me to have a good life. Since birth, it seemed as if I was hit with constant attack. Before being born, I experienced a traumatic and damaging event that started the domino effect of pain that led to my self-esteem being low because I could physically see that I was different. This tragedy happened because of my uncle's irresponsible behavior.

According to the perspectives of my mom and uncle, my mom was moving into her own place, and my uncle decided to help her. My uncle didn't know that my mom was pregnant (his words). As they finished putting away some of the furniture into the apartment, they went back to take in more things. My mom grabbed other items from the truck. She was hovering over it. My uncle, out of spite, concerning a matter that he didn't approve of, then got back into the driver side of the car to proceed to pull off, fully aware that she wasn't sitting stably. He stated that as he was pulling off, the truck jerked, and my mom fell off. My uncle and another relative both thought it was funny. Hearing such words infused anger in my heart towards my uncle. This was my life he played with. Ultimately, he shouldn't have had the opportunity to choose if I lived or died.

The idea that a person believes he/she has the right to take someone else's life is not their decision. God is the creator of life. He has the power to take it away. My uncle, at the time, chose to play God, not considering the consequences of his action. How often in this present time do we see many innocent people or even criminals killed at the hands of someone else playing God?

Statistically, many are killed by someone they know. Jealousy, anger, mental illness, to name a few, are reasons some use to remove a life that God placed here for His glory. Since the time of Cain and Abel, we have seen what happens when sin enters the earth and into the hearts of man. Riddled by jealousy towards his brother, Cain believed he knew better than God. Abel pleased God because he had given Him the best of the fruit from his labor. His heart was pure before God because he knew who set the foundations of the planet he worked on. We are to give God all of ourselves, not just the parts we want Him to fix. Leaning on our own understanding and not trusting that God knows exactly what pleases Him is why Cain fell short of His glory.

Similarly, concerning the incident with my uncle, he had no idea of the plan God had for my life. His decision to question God's reason as to why I was conceived through his brother wasn't a valid reason to act out of anger and nearly take my life. Man may have strategic purposes in his heart, but God determines the ultimate steps. My steps had already been foreordained. Satan, using the mind and hands of my uncle, couldn't take away the seed that had been planted.

To find comedy in the fact that my mom fell off his truck bothered me as his one mistake altered the development of some major organs in my body. There is no humor in what he had done, triggered by feelings of disgust that it was my mother who carried the seed of his brother.

Though filled with hurt from the idea that the enemy used him to bring trauma inside of my mother's womb, I was thankful to God for the information as it led to connecting one of the pieces to my puzzle. I brought the newfound revelation to my mom and asked her for her side of what took place. She confirmed the story and stated that she went home not fixated on the incident until she noticed that she was bleeding from below. She rushed to the hospital to make sure the pregnancy was still stable. To her surprise, she learned from the doctors that she had miscarried and that there was nothing else they could do. What made the story extraordinary to me was that when she returned home and rested for a few days, she felt a kick inside of her stomach. She told my grandmother that she believed she was still pregnant. Going back to the doctors, she was informed that she miscarried a twin, but there was still life inside of her womb: I was still alive. I asked my uncle if my biological dad knew of the situation that occurred, and I was told "no."

Alive and well from the naked eye, Satan could not forfeit the motion for my existence. While continuing to develop until delivery, God covered me. With the one day of channeling ill feelings towards my mother from my uncle, I believed that he knew my mom was pregnant and needed to make a decision since she may not have done it herself. According to my knowledge of him purposefully stepping on the gas, I can assume that he was not happy for his brother. Although he mentioned that my dad wasn't aware of the incident, I still wondered that if my biological father knew such an action had taken place, would he have done something about it? This action had taken place at the hands of one whom he called brother. My emotions suggested that since my biological father had no knowledge of what had taken place or cared to know the result of the incident, my life didn't matter to him. Slipping into the subconscious of my mind with assumption, I could only focus on the reality set forth, not an image that didn't exist. I survived through the completion of my mom's pregnancy.

Months later, on April 10th, 1993, I entered the world. What seemed like a normal day for doctors and nurses that delivered babies turned out to be a battle for my life. This day will be an unforgettable day for my family. When I finally came out, I was placed in the NICU because I wouldn't cry. The doctors didn't provide a full explanation to my mom of the problem but assured her that they would inform her if something else had come up. Before I could fully be released to my mom, she received news that I was being transported to the nearby children's hospital, where the doctors there would give her more information about my transition.

When she finally arrived at the Children's Hospital, she learned that I had an imperforate anus and that I was in surgery. An imperforate anus happens when a child is born with an improperly developed anus. This affects the baby's ability to pass stool normally from the rectum out of their body. The first surgery that is performed by the doctor is a colostomy. A cut is made in the anal area to pull the rectal pouch down into place and create an anal opening (**MedlinePlus Medical Encyclopedia**). Through the surgery, they learned that I was born with only one functioning kidney, and my bladder, which seemed to be in the worst condition, was leaking constantly because my urethra was damaged. The urethra has a muscle that allows the urine to be held. I was in surgery for 12 hours or so before I could finally be with my mom since my birth. The damage to my body was a direct result from the fall my mom endured at the early stages of her pregnancy.

From the time I came out of the womb until the age of nine, I had multiple surgeries intended to fix the problems that were caused by the fall from the truck. I had to wear a colostomy bag for two years before I was able to wear pull-ups. I now call myself the miracle baby. My mother informed me that during these moments in the hospital, there would be times when I stopped breathing. The doctors made my mom believe that I wouldn't live past the age of 2. She told me she was very frightened and believed that she was going to lose me forever. During the time when the doctors told her the struggles with breathing were really bad, she immediately rushed to the hospital. When she arrived, they let her know that I was fine and soon would be going home.

After three weeks or so in the NICU, I was finally able to go home with my mom. Although I was leaving the hospital; the damage had severe repercussions, and for years I was in and out of the hospital because of complications that happened after the surgeries. It seemed that doctors were constantly trying to figure out how to "fix me." God gave my mom the strength to endure, especially since she was only 17 at the time. In my constantly sheltered life of being in the hospital often, the pain was significant because not only did it have an effect on me physically, it also made a huge impact on my mental and emotional state. While I was young and couldn't process what was occurring in my life, God still had a plan.

Later in my life, after talking to my mom about it, she mentioned that the reason the doctors had stopped operating on me was because they believed that my body would heal itself naturally and that they needed some of my organs to fully develop before performing another major surgery. These recurring issues came to an end in March of 2002. I remember that day as I had been in the hospital a few days before being prepared for the major operation that was to take place. It was so vivid to me because I was required to drink a whole gallon of clear water that tastes like iron and death. It's something they give to those who require surgery in order to completely empty the entire intestines. I hated the taste so much that I wouldn't drink it, which the doctors then had to put a tube in my nose in order for me to finish the remaining content. I fought those doctors like crazy, and remember it was about five or six of them because I was so strong. I laugh to this day because an 8 turning 9-year-old girl, was able to fight off so many doctors. Eventually, my strength withdrew, and the tube was placed in my nose.

The day of the surgery was a day that I also remember because I couldn't eat after drinking the iron (that's what I call it). To prepare to be in the surgery room, they attempted to put the anesthesia on my face. The nurse who was with me put bubble gum flavor inside of the mask to mask the smell of iron. To this day, I hate iron (smell, taste, etc.). As the nurse talked to me about having a great sleep, I dozed off. I'm not sure how long the surgery lasted, but I remember waking up in my room and being so sore. I couldn't laugh as hard as I wanted to nor eat anything. I had looked at my stomach because I knew that's where the operation had taken place. There I looked down to see staples and bandages from the middle to the end of my stomach.

I stayed in the hospital for weeks to ensure I had a full recovery with no complications from the surgery. The day before my discharge, I recall helping the doctor to finally take the staples out of my stomach. It was pretty cool at that moment because, little by little, we took each Band-Aid off and removed each staple. I was so happy to finally get the staples out, only to be disappointed by the fact that I couldn't eat regular food and that my body needed more healing, which meant that I would have to take things very slowly before I could go back to my normal life.

It was terrifying. I just wanted to be a kid that didn't live inside of the hospital. To be able to play with friends, go back to school, and do normal kid stuff seemed distant. I missed home cooking. Drinking broth and eating Jell-O was so annoying. This repeated for a few weeks. I took liquids to introduce my body back to normal. As a young girl, I couldn't quite understand that; I figured that once the surgery was over, the life I once knew would reappear. It was also difficult to laugh or turn my body when someone was speaking. I had to be gentle with myself as my body began the healing process.

The day finally came, I was discharged, and able to eat regular food. I was happy to be able to go home because I was tired of the confinements of the hospital. The surgery was a success in that the doctors closed my bladder, and they took part of my large intestines to create a new bladder; for the rest of life, I would have to use a catheter to urinate. The doctor created an opening from my naval that is connected to my bladder. This means that instead of using the bathroom from the bottom, like 95% of the world, I empty out through the naval. Going home, I was relieved because this part of the battle was finally over, and I had gotten the victory. Since then, I have never needed another surgery to correct that part of my body. Over several years, I became more comfortable at using a catheter; but, I was still sheltered due to me not knowing anyone who had the same condition that I did. It felt weird urinating through my belly button. I did indeed have a great childhood since I was able to wear normal underwear, like my peers, and continue with school.

As I grew older, entering the years that boys make it known that they like you, I began to struggle with the insecurity of having to use a catheter. To be quite honest, using the catheter isn't the hardest part of my memories, but going through the belly button is what triggers me emotionally at times when I think about it. I'm so self-conscious that I will not become seriously involved with anyone who accepts being with someone that has my condition. My body is so well hidden; it usually takes years for my friends to find out that the reason why I take such a long time in the restroom is due to the fact that it takes my bladder a little longer to release. I pray that the person God has for me would be comfortable with it. Sometimes it's not easy living with this knowledge. At times it feels like I'm holding some secret that no one is able to know. While even writing this, I'm struggling to realize that this is my life until I enter eternity. At 26, you would think that I've become more confident in my situation, but I want to meet someone who is able to relate to and really understand what I experienced in the first 26 years of my life, of which 17 years is being restricted to using a catheter to release my urine. I am learning, however, that God is able to use this part of my story to inspire someone else to be brave and embrace an imperfection.

Prayer

—∞—

Dear Lord, thank You for creating me to be all that You have called me to be. I have struggled for years to accept the fact that You designed me differently. I toiled with the possibility of You making a mistake in Your design and that I didn't deserve to spend my life with a disability. Why would a loving God make such a drastic decision to create a child whose life may be crippled by the fact of a situation I couldn't change? God, as years went by, I've learned to be content in the destiny You orchestrated for me before the beginning of time. You knew before the foundation of the earth that You would create me with these unique challenges. I've accepted that I'm not a mistake and that my purpose on this present earth shows a loving Christ, sacrificially dying on a cross so that I may have the freedom of living with my condition, bringing glory to Your Holy Name.

To the person with a birth defect: God, I pray for the heart, mind, and spirit of the person reading this part of my book. You have seen the private tears and anguish with being different. The world has looked upon them in shame, making them believe that You made a mistake: what a lie from the devil. Lord, You are the Master Creator and have not made a mistake since the beginning of time. You have made it clear from Genesis chapter one that You created all humans in Your image, and it was good (Genesis 1:26). Lord, let it be known to this person that You have a will and purpose for their life. It is not a mistake that they were brought into the earth. I pray for healing throughout their entire body. Help them to rest in Your promises that You will be the author and finisher of their faith. Bring them peace that surpasses all understanding. Make way for the flood gates to pour out blessings into their lives. As they progress in their journey, allow their light to shine so vibrantly that their disabilities only highlight the good work You did and will continue to do in their lives. Help them to recognize that all ashes which have come from the enemy to steal, kill, and destroy has no match for the cross. Teach them to re-learn their value and to love themselves the way You do. Purpose in their hearts to live out a life totally surrendered to You. Help them see that all battle scars bring life to those who may be struggling to see the beauty in which You created them. I pray that You are glorified, honored and praised, Amen.

Battle Scars

People in society have placed this level of perfection on human beings that they themselves are unable to attain. You have to have the right body type, perfect face, and extreme eating habits. The struggle becomes more unbearable when you have a birth defect. Some of these are visible, such as down syndrome and missing limbs, while some are not unless you're being intimate. Throughout this "normal" that we have no control over, it has been seen as a "curse" because we have tried to box God in believing that we, as humans, have the standard of what God defines as beauty. I have been there, wanting to please the world and hoping that someone would love me despite my shortcomings or lack of beauty impressions. I've learned that those who make it their mission to make someone else feel inadequate because of a condition that they have no control over have major issues internally. To be able to look at someone with disgust because of something they can't change reveals the cruelty of a person's heart. God's Word makes it clear that whatever flows from the heart abundantly comes out of the mouth (Luke 6:45). It saddens me to know that many people choose to commit suicide or simply hide themselves for fear of judgment coming from others. To be honest, with the way the world is set up, society will never proactively allow people with noticeable birth defects to feel like they're of the "norm." There are frustrations that come with having to explain certain things to people because they make assumptions. No one on earth is perfect.

The One I know as perfect took time to create such a beautiful person. I believe that there's a way to not feel pressured or angry with someone because they don't understand or know how to deal with the difficulty of knowing you are different based on what society defines as "beauty." Looking in the mirror. I pray that we can one day be so in love with God that we appreciate the walk He has given us because it displays His majesty. May we know that God doesn't make mistakes and that if someone tells you that you are, know that they are projecting their own insecurities onto you in order to feel better. It's a type of bullying that portrays someone who picks on another due to a "lack."

I was teased for years in Elementary school. As a kid, before the surgery occurred, I was constantly leaking from below due to my condition. I had to wear pull-ups until I was eight years old. The struggle was real at the tender age of 6 or 7. It happened in class where I opened my bookbag to grab something and a classmate saw my pull-up. After school on the bus, I sat down and began to chat with friends. The girl who saw the pull-up in my bookbag asked me to take it out. I obliged at first because I was embarrassed but did it anyway because she persisted. I opened my bookbag, and as I reached for it, she snatched it out of my hand and began waving it in the air. I tried my best to grab it back, but I could hear the laughter from the other kids on the bus. I finally grabbed it from her and put it back in my bag. I don't think I cried as she did that because I didn't grasp the fact that she had just bullied me on the bus. That day, she gave me the name "pee-pee girl." That name haunted me for about a week. I never saw her again. I believe it to be true that God had protected me.

As if this horrific experience wasn't enough, I encountered another emotionally sapping incident a few days later. I was walking to daycare alone. One of the girls who was on the bus at that time saw me walking. She made it her business to say, "Hey "pee-pee girl." I ignored her and kept walking. Fortunately, after that incident took place, I never heard those words again. Despite the immediate sense of seeming relief, those words and the scenarios which took place travelled with me mentally for so many years. I still cringe today thinking about it because the actions of those girls were very hurtful. As God allows these instances to be at the forefront of my mind, I'm being healed. So many things have happened in my life due to my condition, but it has never changed the way the Lord loves me or cares about things concerning my life. This is my therapy that has challenged me to love myself in the way God has intended. I'm no longer afraid to say that my condition cripples me to live a life abundantly. I trust in the God who created me and Jesus who died so that I could be free. Our stories don't just end after we tell them, there are others who will one day be born with a defect, and because of us who have gone before them, God will use our ashes to bring beauty. I always believed that I was the only one in the world facing a medical crisis or any type of crisis, but there were people like me and many others who are in the Living Word.

I found it difficult at first to think that God had placed someone in the Bible with a story to tell from the perspective of one who has a defect. It was brought back to my memory of Jesus once He was crucified. The marks were tattooed into His skin. He had pierced hands and feet. I'm pretty sure that if someone saw Jesus like that today, it would bother them. One thing we could count on is the fact that Jesus had those scars to show us how much He loved us; we can be reminded that scars have value and purpose.

You are a warrior for the kingdom. I look at my scars as tiger stripes knowing that the battle I faced was won like the victory Jesus gained by dying on the cross. The most amazing part about the crucifixion was knowing that Jesus went there on purpose, knowing His body would be scarred. How precious to know that your wounds tell a story of Mercy and Grace. No, we are not Jesus, but He gave us a story of our own to share with the world. Battle scars are proof that despite the attacks that come your way, you can handle it because you have always been a fighter. Even when we feel as if there is no more fight within us, we somehow find the strength to courageously say, "I'll try this one last time and then succeed." Life, in itself, is a battle every single person has to finish; for some of us, our fight just started a little earlier. I look up to God, knowing that someday, I'll meet more people in this lifetime who either have the same struggle I've experienced or share a common understanding of how God displays beauty on all levels. I will wear my stripes accordingly and cherish those people in my life who have supported me through the process, as well as came into my life and didn't scrutinize me because of something I inevitably can't change. I'll leave this golden nugget with you: God sees and hears everything concerning your life.

My brother/sister, God knew you before you were placed in your mother's womb. Having a birth defect of any sort is traumatizing. You tend to feel alone and think that no one will understand the constant mental battle, thinking that God made a mistake when He designed you. The light at the end of the tunnel may seem infinitely distant. It is those moments when it seems so much easier to live out in defeat because using strength and perseverance seems tedious. We must learn to hold on to the fact that God knew exactly what He was doing and that if we surrender our lives to Him, that our story will transform the life of someone else.

I often struggle with the thought that my condition may stop me from being a mom or wife. It cripples me sometimes to know that this is the walk that God chose for me. Did He know I was going to struggle with this? Absolutely! He knew you would as well. It is the enemy's job to keep what we think as weaknesses to enable us to be used for the Kingdom of God. Endless times, I've "been in my feelings," questioning God as to why He created me like this? To this day, I am yet to come to that full understanding; but, I carry this hope and peace that I will meet others like myself, and it will no longer feel as though I'm carrying this burden alone. Being a unique individual is not a curse.

In my heart, I believe God does some amazing things with people who stand out from among the crowd. From this day forward, let's be thankful that despite our conditions, God has brought us through, and we are living our lives for His glory. I empathize with you, and I Love You. More importantly, God loves you in a way that I can never. Be vigilant in your pursuit of Him, knowing that despite what uncontrollable situation you face, the fact that you woke up this morning is a testament that God is not through. Take a deep breath, look at yourself in the mirror, and speak the true words of life that come from God's Word. Some days it will be easier to look in the mirror; other days, the tears will flood. We are not a mistake. The battle scars we picked up in whichever way we did will not stop the plan God has for us. For those of you that are bitter with your condition, revisit those wounds and submit to the authority of Christ. The victim mentality gets us nowhere. It causes us to find fault in a perfect God. One who knew that the world would make you feel deeply ashamed for a change you may not be able to fix. Rest in the fact that Jesus understands your pain in a way that no other human can. Jesus has been there: left alone because He stood out from among the crowd. He had the courage to face opposition and say, "God's will be done." His scars remind us of the work at the cross, and He chose to show Thomas, the disciple, His wounds. He will be there for you always; just trust in Him. Lean not on your own understanding but acknowledge God in all your ways. In this hope, we know that He is directing our paths (Proverbs 3:5-8).

Prayer

Heavenly Father,

    Today, I pray for the one you called to stand out. Living in a place where differences are frowned upon isn't easy. The gift of carrying such a load feels, at times, like a burden. Fighting to constantly make others understand isn't the idea You had in mind when You created the gift reading this book, but here they are. I pray that they would have eyes to see and ears to hear what 'thus said the Lord.' Your word is clear in stating that each of us are fearfully and wonderfully made. This means no mistakes were present when You formed us in our mother's womb. I pray for healing over their mind, body and soul. Ease the tension of wanting to be perfect, for You are the only one who is perfect. Thank You for taking the time to create such a precious individual. May they never forget the Master Creator as the source of true Beauty, Amen.

Rated PMG (Toxic)

"Daddy issues" is something I typically don't address because not having a father in my life didn't faze me until I became an adult. Knowing who my father was but not really focusing on the lack of involvement allowed me to live a life where coming from a one-parent home was the latter. Parental Misguidance stood out among the mess disguised as love between children and parent(s). As I was writing the book, I realized that I could spend so many hours talking about having a toxic mom because my biological father wasn't around. I noticed that oftentimes, I saw a lot of men come into the lives of my siblings and I, having no intentions except getting what they wanted from my mother. Growing up witnessing different men make their way into our home without much concern for the fact that my brothers and I desperately needed a male figure in our lives was a traumatizing experience.

One thing was always for sure! I got to see my mom sell her worth with each person she allowed to cross that door. I remember as a kid being woken up in the middle of the night to hear my mom and a man having sex. Too young to fully grasp the idea that was typical adult behavior, I took it as a sign deep down in my spirit to not trust any man. I don't recall ever being introduced to them. The only person I always heard was my mother. A child should never be exposed to such an event that it costs them their livelihood. I didn't want to be like that. I honestly didn't know what I actually wanted. Outside of hearing my mom in the middle of the night, I recall around the age of 7 or 8 when I witnessed a man put his hand on my mother for the first time.

We were all sitting in the living room when a fight broke out. My mom was able to defend herself to a certain point, but the man eventually overpowered her. I remember my first brother and I throwing things, like forks, at him to get his attention to stop. Eventually, he did, but the repercussions that soon followed appeared as he ran out of the house, and my mom sat up with a swollen eye shut and a bloody nose. Horrified, my mom called the police to document what had taken place. For weeks, she lost the ability to see out of one eye. We watched her every day for quite some time, putting a warm towel on her eye to expedite healing the damages. Eventually, it did. We showed so much excitement that her eye went back to normal, but the imagery of that day left an imprint in my mind that pushed me to not trust men even more. That man never had another opportunity to hurt us as a family.

Watching these toxic relationships play out really helped me to be more cautious when dealing with guys sexually. I made a vow to myself that I would never allow a man to use me for sex like my mom did with those men and how those men did with my mom. A vicious cycle that still haunts me in my adult life. I don't know if having my father in my life would have made a difference in the lifestyle I was watching in the home. With this going on in my personal life, I had three options to choose from regarding a relationship with men:

1. Become promiscuous
2. Become a homosexual woman
3. Trust my gut to know that one day I would meet a man who wouldn't be like the men I saw growing up.

I chose number three. Now, don't get me wrong, I struggled in my youth and young adult life to have a Godly relationship with men. The dosage of pain I saw as a child crept up on me as I became an adult. Broken relationships, before I could even open my eyes to the world we live in, set off a motion in Satan's mind. The Word tells us that his job is to kill and destroy. What better way to do that than to bring a child into a world with a broken family?

Statistics show that when children grow up without a father, it places a heavy burden on their heart and leaves a void. Although a number of children are blessed to have a stepdad who may enter their lives, the hole placed by the lack of presence of their biological father leaves repercussions that sometimes carry into our adult lives. I have met countless friends, especially men, who, because of the lack of a male presence in their lives, have a hard time understanding themselves and building great relationships with women. Most have been raised in a single-parent home where mom truly lacks the full understanding of how to raise a man because she failed to lean on God for guidance. I have seen this struggle, especially in my own house with three brothers.

My mom didn't show us how to have a great relationship with any type of male figure because she didn't have it herself. The men that did come into our lives were never there to stay; they just used my mom like a bookshelf that collected dust and can only be pulled when they felt like it. I hated it because I saw so much emotional and physical abuse. A seed had been sown in my heart to hate men because of what I saw on a daily basis. I honestly don't think my mom knew how much pain she caused her children with these actions. I didn't realize that my father not being around would twist my outlook on relationships with men.

During the days of constantly being pricked from needles and receiving only support from my mom while going through a childhood; spent 85% of that time in the hospital. I often wondered where my biological dad was. My mind was plagued with questions like: did he know all the things that were going on in my life? Does he love me? And many others. While my mom didn't really mention him or share many memories she had of him, on some occasions, I would see him hanging outside of the store with some other men in a wheelchair. I learned years later that my dad was a drug dealer. He owed someone money, and to make a "statement," he was shot in the back. It paralyzed him from the waist down. I don't believe telling me this information at a young age would have bothered me as much but knowing it as an adult really made me feel like I missed out on showing compassion for what took place.

I know one thing for sure though, when I did see him outside of the store, I would be so thrilled to see him. I remember finally getting a telephone number from him to contact him at any time. I called often and talked with him, but the impact was so little. I would always have to reach out in order to speak. I don't even remember the last conversation we had or the last time I saw his face. I just knew that the conversations had ceased, and I didn't ask anyone why he didn't come around. For years after, it seemed as though I was missing or lacking a part of myself. As I got older and saw my friends having both parents around and they were in communication with their fathers, I thought about my dad even more. I guess not having him around really made a difference. A father is supposed to be a girl's "first love." Having this separation had already broken my heart before any other man could. God is clear about both parents raising children. Whether we like to admit it or not, a father's presence is necessary for both genders. Deep in my subconscious, I longed for my dad. Lack of communication from him brought numbness. Did I really need him? This gaping hole in my heart left me even more sheltered and abandoned.

I will, however, say that although my dad wasn't present, his mom was. For about the first nine years of my life, I was always close to my paternal grandma. She always wanted me around; and, during those times with her, I never saw my dad. I never asked her about him when she would come to pick me up; but I often wonder now that I'm older if she would have been able to ease any pain that I felt because of his abandonment. After my surgery was completed, I lost contact with her, and things began to seem normal for a change even without the presence of my other parent. My childhood had regained some of its kid-friendly times. I began to block out the thought that my dad would one day come around, and I would get to know that side of him.

In 2004, the time came when, even in my adult life, if I wanted to know my dad, the opportunity to do so was no longer available. We were sitting outside in the school yard when my cousin came up to me and said my name was in the newspaper. At first, I didn't want to know why, but deep in my soul, I knew that I needed to take a look. I took the newspaper and started to read. It was there because my dad had passed away. No one came and told me about it; I didn't know how to feel at that moment, so I brushed it off and gave the newspaper article back to my cousin. That day runs so deep in my subconscious that the reason why I was able to discuss it is because it is a part of my story. I didn't tell my mom the news when I got home. Because of the fact that my dad wasn't present in my life, it was easy to forget that he no longer existed. What a terrible place to be as a child. There were no tears to shed, and the thought of actually having any type of sorrow ceased to have a place in my heart. This event made 'forgetting I had a dad' normal. With the troubles I saw in the men who did cross paths, I got accustomed to not having a strong male presence in my life. I believed that they all had the same mentality, and each of them caused more harm than good.

As I reflect, as an adult, on the fact that my dad wasn't present, I realize that I needed him. I will never get the opportunity to have a conversation with my dad because he passed away. I really wanted to know him more and maybe have an understanding of some parts of myself that could have come from his side. I did, however, learn from one of my aunts that at times, when I was small, my dad would try to come around, but my mom forbade him. My mom figured since he didn't have any money to spare, he didn't deserve to spend time with me. Having this revelation hurts because money should never be the driving focus when it comes to a relationship with a father.

I vowed that my children would always know their father. I wouldn't dare come in between their relationship. Marriage is definitely the goal to achieve this purpose. So often, women become bitter because a man may move on or may not be able to provide for the child as they see fit. This is such troubling waters because, honestly, I grew angry as she never talked about it. How could she be a part of removing such a pivotal person from my life? I have yet to tell her how I feel about the information. Her actions for some parts of my life have really revealed to me the importance of having a relationship with Christ before pursuing any relationship. Channeling feelings of resentment and inadequacy, I couldn't help but think that there was a reason for the choice behind her decision. Time in gaining details on her thought processes reeled in as I got older.

We spend so much time as a society dwelling on the fact that people who lack having their biological fathers in their life have daddy issues in the future. One topic we always miss the mark on is the fact that unfit mothers exist as well. I struggled internally, deciding if it is appropriate to discuss the condition of my mother's sanity, which caused layers of trauma to deeply impact my life. Because a woman carries the child in her womb, enduring the changes in her body, as well as sorrow in childbirth, we give praise to the commitment she has made. I don't use that sentence as an excuse but as a reality check that some women shouldn't have become mothers. A conversation with a friend put this mental battle in perspective: God uses whatever vessel He desires to bring forth His purpose. I questioned how it was desirable to use a woman with mental instability as a tool for carrying children. However, I looked upon it, God had done what He wanted, and here I was to bring Him glory.

The perspective that shook me to my core ignited a fire in me to understand my mother's illness and how I could still honor her despite feeling as though she failed me as a parent. The stigma revolving around mental illness in the Black community has been the "hush-hush" of all time. Believing that it's best to be silent while a person grapples with imbalance that they have no control over. In society, we put forth the energy to address the signs of something "wrong" in a child that we forget to analyze a reality that that child will one day become an adult: the adult with an illness from childhood. As many shall read this book, I find it in my heart to not disclose what illness my mother is battling, but to give sight into the notion that children of the women/men with such challenges have an overwhelming inkling to shove the idea of building a strong connection with the one who brought them here in the back of their mind. Knowing that formulating relationships simply can't always be possible due to the blockage of undiscovered reality that a parent is fighting between delusion and actuality, pushes the limits to be more compassionate. Shaping the heart to reflect Christ is challenging me to see my mom as human. Superwoman tendencies from early on had been a belief the world made me think all women possessed. The woman who gave birth to me is human, and as difficult as it is at times to understand her, I'm striving to love even when the brokenness cuts like a knife.

The pressure to deal with daddy issues was just one instance, whereas, missing the emotional connection with my mom as well tends to bring up even more insecurities. My mom had always been emotionally disconnected from me. I don't recall in my childhood receiving any hugs and kisses frequently. Sure, sometimes this would happen; but, not having that as a child caused me to look for it in the future in the wrong places. With full awareness of the condition in her life, I've come to understand the possibility that she may never be able to have the mother-daughter relationship I always pictured. It has settled in my heart to be conscious of this part of my life and to move with the intent of maintaining peace when chaotic episodes present themselves. I love my mom, and as hard as it is to deal with someone fighting a battle of that magnitude, I cherish the thought that some of her days as a child, teenager or adult had some sense of normalcy. Memories in such moments are trapped in the deep parts of my mind, ready to appear when I need a reminder that I have seen times as a youth that don't remind me of an illness.

Before becoming the person I know today, I could remember that mom was a party goer and smoked as well as drank often with different people. We lived with my grandmother most of the time. My mom had me at 17 and my first brother at 19. Still a teenager with two children, I believe that the reason why I saw this growing up is because my mom had missed part of her years due to becoming a parent. Her last two children came in her 20s, but that didn't stop her from doing the usual. I agree that a child should be born despite the age of the parent, but my mom's focus was still enjoying her youth, even with two children at home. While growing up, I remember her stories of going out and leaving my brother and I alone at home. I was a toddler at the time, and when she would come back home, she said I would be dressed already, and I was in the process of getting him dressed. I figured that before the "change" occurred that really altered our reality, my mom had already shown us some type of neglect for personal reasons.

Moving back into the idea that society doesn't really talk about unfit mothers, I have grown into the knowledge that coming from a completely broken home, where my dad wasn't there emotionally or physically, and my mom not being there emotionally, shaped my oftentimes controlling ways. I desire to have some type of control over my life. Coming face to face with the reality that I'm honestly not in control of anything puts me at ease. I long for hugs and kisses (not from my mom, though). I mentally blocked out the thought that she would one day be emotionally available to me. We have to get to a place, especially in the Church, where it's not always about the fact that a child is being raised in a one-parent home. Sometimes that one-parent home is not comfortable or safe. Going outside was my way of coping even as a child. I had an understanding that I shouldn't have had because innocence should be just that: innocence.

My great-grandfather told me at the age of 10 that I was wise beyond my years. Though it was a compliment at such a tender age, the reality was that I was growing up before I could even process who I am. Placing such a burden on a child to learn how to cope emotionally really breathes control issues in the future. I would always do my best to "try" and control my situations, although it was to no avail. I was struggling with the fact that people who were older than me could have so much power over my life. It didn't register to me until I was older to know that a person had either mentally or emotionally controlled who I was—linking it back to the idea that this stemmed from not being in control of what happened to my mom. It took my world by storm, carrying heavy debris as I lay broken with no idea of how to recover. My innocence of childhood had come to an end; the adult version of myself to keep my brothers and I sane took place.

Due to being the oldest of my siblings, my controlling ways settled in as I took on the role of "mom." Yes, my mom was present physically, but I could tell that her mind wasn't the same. She began to say things like, "The Government has a chip in our heads controlling our every movement." It caught me off guard because I couldn't understand why she was saying these things. This revelation appeared after she broke the glass mirror in the bathroom and locked us inside by placing the couch behind the door. I was lost. On top of this crisis my family was enduring, I was also at the age where my hormones had come full-blown. With a monthly cycle coming in, my irrationality came along also. Frantically, trying to make sense of dealing with my mom, I became angry. I walked with a chip on my shoulder, daring anyone who came close to try and break it down. The antics just didn't stop there. In the back of my mind, I wondered if my family knew what was going on. So many questions began to formulate in my mind. Who was this new person I called mom? While channeling my own thoughts of the crisis we were facing, I wanted so badly to believe that this was just a dream.

The background knowledge needed to understand the change that occurred in my mom didn't fully manifest until I entered further into my teen years. I knew that something had taken place, but I wasn't sure what happened. My childhood, between the ages of birth until the age of 11, had its share of highs and lows. Despite being in the hospital so often, I was able to spend a lot of time outside playing with friends and embracing my youth. My mom parented the way most parents did in the 90's. Kids were allowed to hang outside every day after school and all day on the weekends. Like most of us who grew up in the 90's, we had that one rule: be home before the streetlights came on. We didn't worry about if we would be kidnapped or if any trouble was lurking ahead; neither a warning was shared. Everyone knew each other in the neighborhood. I'm not sure if this was just a southern thing, but it was nearly impossible for me to do something wrong without my mom or grandma finding out about it. It was like a village in which everyone held accountability for one another.

I was a tomboy during this part of my life; so, being dressed in shorts, t-shirts, and sneakers were my thing. I enjoyed hanging out with the boys. They weren't too uptight about little things. I didn't like hanging out with girls because they cared too much about their nails and hair; I, on the other hand, just wanted to have fun. I played football and basketball. Tag, hide/seek, and Simon-says were some of the games that we played in the streets or in someone's driveway. You could always hear laughter throughout the streets.

The summertime, when school was out, was always my favorite time of year. We didn't have to stress about homework; we were able to fully indulge in the carefree spirits of our youth. We didn't quite understand the life of an adult. Oftentimes, we as children were so eager to grow up and become adults. I'm not sure why that was ingrained in our brains, but it was. I enjoyed the carefree life: one that I believe at that time would last forever. I didn't think that pain and sorrow could ever cross our paths. My focus was on spending time outside because I had missed so much of it. While going through a child-life crisis, having this normalcy couldn't compare to being stripped of my adolescence through the mental breakdown my mom, my younger siblings and I experienced. The mental challenges that burst through our front door came with no warning; no one in the neighborhood prepared us for the fact that the lives of my siblings and I were about to be disrupted before we could fully grasp the idea that the mom we knew had gone to a faraway place and this "new person" had emerged.

Traumatized by the danger lurking in the atmosphere of the Colonial Trace apartments in New Orleans, a battle my soul couldn't triumph on its own appeared because I wasn't aware that I was fighting a war with the supernatural using physical weakness. Ephesians 6:12 describes to the believer that the fight between good and evil is spiritual, and Ephesians 6:11 requires the use of the full armor of God. Yet, here I was at the tender age of 11, trying to destroy giants that I couldn't see or hear.

While listening to my inner gut tell my fight or flight response to kick in, it seemed like chasing freedom was inevitable. Running was the only answer I found as my faulty solution. Racing to the finish line that hadn't been created, pulled back into the perilous moment when I walked inside the apartment in New Orleans. The usual sounds of laughter and joy escaping the lips of youth was music to the beat that rummaged through my mind as my brother, and I decided to take an unprecedented break for water. We never walked back home when taking a break from being outside with friends, we always ran. It was like we needed to get back to our place outside before the show began: kind of like when there is a commercial break, and you try your hardest to use the bathroom and get snacks before whatever you were watching came back on. The expectation was like any other day as we went back and forth between outside and inside. If you grew up in the 90s, you would hear after the second time, "You come back in this house again, and you're not going back out." Though that was true for my brother and I on numerous occasions, we were not prepared for the twisted version of life to send us running for safety from the brewing storm knocking at the door. The trials we faced in a moment of time's notice didn't depict the final say God orchestrated in years to come.

My brother and I walked into our home, and our lives did a complete 180 degrees turn. As we walked up the stairs, we were met with one of the women who lived on the same floor as us with the words, "everything will be okay." With no idea of what she was talking about, we went inside to take a break because we had been outside all day. Deep in my relocation, I can't remember if my mom was there when we walked in or if she was in the bathroom. We both walked in and heard glass shattering. Moments later, my mom went into the kitchen and grabbed a broom to clean up the mess. Unsure of why, all of a sudden, she finished cleaning the bathroom, came up front, and then placed the couch behind the door. I don't recall hearing her say anything in between the time; I could have just blocked it out from my memory. When she put the couch behind the door, it became evident to my brother and I that we wouldn't be going outside. This ordeal lasted for at least a week until one night, my grandmother and her husband came to the apartment and woke us up to leave.

The next few weeks were a blur, but my mom wasn't the same person I remembered. Her actions changed; it was like dealing with a side I didn't quite understand. My grandma didn't explain most of it to us, I believe, because she didn't understand it herself. My mom came to visit us from time to time, and when my grandma would take us places, she'd stop by a bridge. This was the current living situation my mom was in: homeless and living under the bridge. Watching this unfold with no clarity, I just knew this was the "new" normal mom. She was finally able to secure another apartment, taking my brothers and I away from family until the events of Hurricane Katrina.

Living with her was a nightmare. She was emotionally disconnected. The apartment was a one-bedroom; so, we shared a living space with my mom, all four children cramped up with her. I would go into the living room as a way to get a break because we couldn't go outside. No one from our family came to see how we were doing. Occasionally, my grandma tried, but nothing changed because my mom was determined to live as she pleased. We transferred schools as well due to what had happened mentally. It was a constant struggle because I just wanted things to go back to how they were; and, going through my own hormonal changes didn't help either. Being stuck inside all day with no other human interaction made me very angry with her. I developed a cold heart and shoulder. I was deeply hurting on the inside and had no release or escape. For one year, I came face to face with mental illness.

We were sheltered, abused, and neglected because people would rather push those with mental illnesses to the side instead of trying to find ways of helping. I often heard family members who lived where we lived tell us that someone slipped a "mickey" in her drink. My interpretation of a "mickey" was that someone had severely drugged her, which left her unable to ever bounce back from it. My siblings and I never got the full context of what happened to my mom, but I knew that dealing with someone who suffers from a mental illness is not easy. It breaks up relationships.

To this day, I still don't fully comprehend the illness that affects my mom, but I strive to learn more about it so that it helps me not take what she does personally. Although her state of mind brings toxicity to my life, I've learned to choose the battle I fight when she is not herself. For years, I tried to escape this reality when the rough moments were just too much to bear. I wanted so badly to help; but, running away from it felt like the best response. I constantly struggle with being emotionally connected to my mom. Some days are easier than others; but, I have found that our relationship works better from a distance. She has shared in some moments that she has a chemical imbalance and can't control how she feels when she wakes up. It doesn't change how badly it impacts my relationship with her. I often pray that I don't have the same issues that she does. I push myself daily to be aware of my emotions and how I'm feeling. It's not easy, especially when a sister-girl comes for her monthly visit.

In this day and age, dealing with my mom has become slightly easier. I won't say that we have the best relationship, but I try. God has definitely helped me come to terms with the fact that I can release my controlling mechanisms and embrace His authority to have His will for my life. He has given me the ability to see my mom as she is and to know that with His guidance as my Loving Father, I can deal with all things that this present life gives me.

One thing I know for sure is that it breaks my heart to know that we, as a community, especially the Christian community, don't talk about mental illness and how it impacts the lives of those who are close to it. Through my studies, I've discovered that God addressed mental illness in the Bible, for example, the man in Matthew 8. The Bible describes him as constantly crying in the caves, fighting, but not knowing that the fight is within himself, so he cuts through his body, hoping that somehow it can ease the pain. His day came the moment that Jesus stepped out of the boat into his community. This man seeking freedom from anything or anyone, ran up to Jesus as if any ounce of hope left over could finally be used for this very moment.

For years, the way that society dealt with his issue was to outcast him and chain him like an animal. He was worthless in their eyes because they didn't know how to address his needs. To chain someone without acknowledging the humanity side of it showed that the people had little to no compassion for this man. Honestly, we don't fully understand how mental illness correlates to dealing with the demonic. We place blame on the parent of the child or adult. Every single person that God has allowed to walk this earth has battled demons: some internally, some externally. In many cases, people deal with both. I, for one, watch it happen with my own eyes, seeing demonic spirits overtake someone who has no idea that this is their "new" normal. Are we, as a church, even equipping ourselves to deal with such issues?

We see many people in society who are homeless, dealing with mental illness. The way we have dealt with it was to laugh at it, shame it, and negligently walk by it without addressing it. I have been guilty of this, but facing it often when dealing with my mom has put things into perspective.

Prayer

Abba,

You are the true Father who art in Heaven. I pray for the weary who is burdened with the battle to honor their earthly parents despite how they received treatment from them. It is so easy to develop a heart of resentment because pain allows the victim mentality. Sulking in a place of bitterness gives way for the enemy to destroy our lives. Some have lost the desire to build a relationship with one or both parents. Others simply don't know the words to say to rekindle a once beautiful relationship. You have asked us to forgive as You have forgiven us. Breathe life into the relationships between children and parents. For those of us who believe reconciliation is not possible at the moment, give us the drive to understand with the intent to be compassionate. Thank You for being our Father. May You be glorified, honored and praised, Amen

.

Poem: Words I can't express

Intro: We live in a world that spends so much time focused on Daddy issues that we don't talk about the fact that toxic Moms can be just as detrimental. This piece is personal; I'm ready to shine light on something the church should invest more time in talking about.

You broke me before my history could be written. Lies escaping the lips of one that I should have put my trust in.

Burning from the inside as the tears roll down my face. I can't cry because like tissue, they have gone to waste.

I needed you at the tender age of time, I rewind some of the memories trapped in blurred lines.

Ones that show a mom whose love should caress the soul of a child whose reflection looks like hers.

No words, just pictures. I imagine that someday I could look into your eyes and tell you that you have been wise in how you have approached me.

You see, I remembered a time long ago when my sorrows and woes didn't exist. And like my hair filled with twist, the pain unraveled in a capsule that no man captured.

The world has been so clear that daddy issues exist, but what about the ones where mom has missed…

Hugs, kisses, packed lunches and granted wishes.

Mom, I'll do the dishes while you entertain a man who doesn't love you.

I'll cook dinner and wash my brother because you're with your new book.

Sure, I'll clean and clean and pray that for once, I don't lean on the understanding that my mom is not present.

Physically here but emotionally distant, how can I grow into a woman when the leader is missing?

Wounds upon wounds that fester in my insides, I can't cry but can't dry my eyes.

Mom why? Tell me you love me, but your actions said otherwise.

I'm broken, heart torn open, looking for air, but my lungs can't focus.

I need you to teach me how to be a woman, not chase a man whose goal is to landslide like I'm some dummy.

Mummy, mum, mom, can you hear me? This world is cold, and my heart is freezing.

Like ice, the pain becomes numb. Like a sore thumb, my head goes thump.

Against the wall, I fall like raindrops. Tell me where you are.

You're supposed to be my star; a shining armor, but the battle that I'm facing isn't glamorous.

It's disastrous, breaking apart at the seams of the being that you carried in your womb, I'm dead on the inside like a tomb.

Whom you brought into the circle of life, where strife and pain poppers give you the knife,

Cut, bled through, seeping out like water, crystal clear and sky blue.

The sadness is thickening, I need you to be the woman that God called you to be; one whose soul has been set free.

I beg you, mom, look into my eyes and say this will end because I'm tired of fighting the demons that confuse me within.

Poem: Words I Can't Express

I'm your daughter, ready to run into your arms and tell you to think smarter, go harder for the one who gave you the name.

Sit me down and tell stories, I promise I won't look with shame.

I love you, adore your existence, love me like you're supposed to, not be at a distance.

Time is running out when I leave you alone, I won't come home or pick up the phone.

You'll be a distant memory as moments have faded, I promise I won't turn back as my spirit has waded, the water of perilous times, sour like limes,

No more crossing silver lines, that's fine, but mom, it's up to you to unwind the damage that has caused me anguish.

Learn my love language. Physical and Quality, not Quantity over a false personality.

Leave that man be, he's no good, just an ole street nigga from the hood. Tales like fairies buried in fantasies, I'm on my knees begging you, please.

Look at me and see my cries, pleas for help, don't leave me with scars that are pelting me with welts. I yelp and whimper because I'm empty on the inside.

Sometimes I don't have emotions, but my anger stretches wide. I hide the sadness, I hide the madness, but eventually, it has to be released.

Singing out like a caged bird, but the words that echo don't sound so sweet.

Meet me where I am and tell me that you love me, meet me where I am, and hug me.

Let me breathe your air because I'm living a beautiful nightmare. Eyes aware but staring into the blank expression on your face.

I'll need space but at the same time want to share your space.

This race isn't for the short and swift, so mom, I'll be waiting, hoping this won't keep causing us to drift.

I won't settle for less, I'll give it my best and look to God so I can pass my test. I'll rest... assured that I'll be a mom one day and I'll look into my daughter's eyes and won't run away.

Make promises to her that I will always keep, remind her that her presence in my life is sweet.

I'll hug, kiss and love her with all my being, because I don't want to leave a void caused by my ignorance and fill her with broken dreams.

She'll know that mom is always there with a listening ear, she will know that I'm near.

I pray for and with her, tell her amazing stories and mom, I want you to know that she won't have to worry.

No sorrows or woes but I'll play little miss piggy with her little toes. And I'll count to ten when she's hiding in place, then she will know I'll come find her at any given place.

She'll hold on to my words that mommy loves her dearly and the people around her will see that clearly.

You have taught me such a tough reality, and one truth will stand, one daughter or two will know that their life is not a fatality.

The Storm

2004 was a trying year, and 2005 had a storm lurking in the water. Before diving into the storm, at the age of 11, I no longer knew who my mom was. It had appeared to be a normal day of going outside to hang out with my friends who lived in the neighborhood; but, later during the night, it turned crazy due to a change in my mom that had occurred of which I was unaware of. I had just begun my 6th-grade year at Harriet Tubman in New Orleans, Louisiana. I was excited because I was graduating again; and, this time, I was going to middle school the following year.

During this stage in life, I was just an innocent, 11-year-old girl having fun with my classmates, who possessed no cares in this world, living freely. I had gotten through several surgeries, the death of my dad even though I didn't know him, and the skies were clearer. Dark clouds and stormy weather headed to the front door of our apartment complex called "Colonial Trace" in New Orleans. It was a day when my brother and I had just come from playing outside. We walked into an apartment where my mom had just broken a glass mirror in our apartment bathroom. She moved the couch behind the door and stopped us from going outside. I didn't understand what was going on, but it got worse and worse as many people kept saying to us, "it's going to be okay, and don't worry about it." I was really confused. I mean, what 11-year-old clearly comprehends such dramatic change is happening in their life?

I had no idea that the innocence of my childhood was about to turn into a nightmare because of something gruesome happening to my mother. From that day forward, for one year, we were not allowed to go outside. My mom's reasoning was that the government had brainwashed us. Slowly, the good memories that I had of my mom were fading as a new person emerged from her. For one week or so, we didn't go outside or have any contact with someone from our family. I guess my maternal grandmother heard what had happened. My grandma stayed in the same apartment complex as us at the time; and, one night, I remember her coming to wake my brothers and I up to tell us that we were going to stay at her house. As we walked out of the door, I looked back to see my mom being cornered by two men in police uniforms and her screaming "Mom, Mom, Mom" repeatedly. Over the next few days, I didn't see my mom, and I was still in shock because it didn't feel right.

After this night, periodically, my mom randomly came to my grandma's house to bring us money for the things we needed. During this time, my mom was homeless and slept outside under a bridge. The feelings I had during those days are locked away in the back of my mind. I guess my brain figured that the event was too traumatic to remember. We lived with my grandmother for a few months before my mom finally got back on her feet and found a new apartment to reside in.

I was scared because I didn't recognize who this new mom was, and I wasn't sure what to expect while living with her again. From the time we moved back in with my mom, we began to suffer from physical and emotional abuse through her words and hands. She took my younger brother and I from Harriet Tubman because she believed that we were being beaten by the teachers and didn't want to tell her. I remember coming home one day, and my mom beat my brother and I until we falsely confessed that we were being beaten at school. After she took us out of that school, the abuse continued for days and months. My brother and I were beaten for no reason at all. Sometimes, she forcefully grabbed a vacuum cleaner stick, held us down, and beat us. We developed lumps on our behinds and were unable to really sit properly because we were in so much pain.

The Storm

Another night she woke us up, accusing us of letting someone into the house to rape her. I was terrified as she held a big knife to both of our throats. Courageously, I stepped in front of my brother, being settled with the thought that she would take me out first because I was the oldest and cared for him. As my brother and I suffered abuse from my mom, I became very angry with my family members because they left us alone and didn't try to "save us." I had no one to call on because my mom restricted us from calling any family members. I felt like this pain would go on and on. It was devastating because we couldn't tell anyone what was going on. I couldn't comprehend the trauma I was facing, but I knew that I had to make a decision that would be way beyond my comfort zone. I made a plan with my brother to run away from my mom since no one else came to help us out. For some reason, I knew where my grandmother had lived, and it registered in my brain to go to her for safety. I never remembered the day or time we left, but I knew it was August of 2005.

After days of planning our escape, my brother and I packed some clothes. We didn't have any money; therefore, we knew that we would have to walk to my grandma's house. My brother and I were used to walking on that street anyway because we used to travel that route when we attended Harriet Tubman. The next day after packing up our clothes, we quietly and safely woke up in the wee hours of the morning, took our things, and began walking to my grandmother's home. I don't think my brother and I talked during that time, and I don't recall how I was feeling. I know for sure I was very scared when we left the house because my mom could have easily woken up and caught us. It would have probably been hell to pay for that swift decision, but I believed God was there with us the entire time and guided us to make sure that we were safe.

We finally reached the street my grandma lived on and hoped that we had made the right decision. We walked up to the door and knocked a few times. No one came to the door; thus, we began to turn around. Suddenly, my grandma called out to us; we were so relieved that she had answered, and we wouldn't have to face the repercussions by returning home. My grandma was so shocked that we were there, but she didn't turn us away. We were with her for a few days, and I even started Middle School. All of that was about to change again because Hurricane Katrina was brewing in the Gulf of Mexico. The news reports predicted the Hurricane to be a tropical storm. Days later, we learned that Hurricane Katrina was a Category 5, and a State of Emergency was declared for Louisiana. Here it was, my brother and I packing up again so that we could go to Texas with my grandma.

August 24, 2005, the day before Hurricane Katrina, most of my family members and I were on our way to Texas, where my aunt lived. When we got there, most of my family was under one roof: 70 people, including children, babies, and adults. It was fun being around my cousins and family again. They asked us questions about what happened and how we felt about the things occurring in our lives. I wanted so badly to just express my frustrations, but the words stuck inside didn't seem to have a voice. We did learn that my mom decided to stay back and not leave for Hurricane Katrina with my two youngest brothers. I don't remember if I missed my mom or not during that time, but my grandma did tell my brother and I that she was pretty upset that we had left her. I guess she didn't understand the trauma she allowed us to encounter due to her actions.

I believed while in Texas that my life was going to get better, considering I was away from my mom. My brother and I even started to attend school in Texas. My family figured since Hurricane Katrina had caused so much damage, we would be moving to Texas unless the State of Louisiana determined that we were allowed back into the city.

For a few weeks, my brother and I enjoyed the company of our family and the relief that we were going to be safe. About two weeks into our stay in Texas, my mom somehow was able to hop on a bus to Texas and come to my aunt's house. It was very sad because she wasn't in her right state of mind and the problems we were facing at home began to resurface. It got to a point that her actions impacted other members of our family.

One night while all of us young children were preparing for bed, my mom's imbalance kicked in. She was just ranting and raving about nothing. One of my older cousins went outside to calm her down so that the rest of the family could sleep. It was so embarrassing. Through her constant up and down of moods to thinking that our family was the enemy, it was too much to take for a now 12-year-old. My nightmare erupted again as she told us that we were only staying in Texas for just a few more days and heading to Omaha, Nebraska. I was nervous because I didn't know how to respond to her words. One of my aunts asked me if I wanted to stay, and I said yes. I mean, I tried so hard to get away from her just for her to come back and remove us from my family. I begged to stay; but, most of my family members, including my grandma, believed that they had no control over the situation because my mom had full custody of us, and she was allowed to do with us as she pleased, as we were minors. My brothers and I were on the move again, far away from our family. We took a bus all the way to Omaha, Nebraska. I'm not sure how many days that was, but when we got there, we lived in a hotel, and reality set in that I would not be seeing my family for a long time.

Prayer

Heavenly Father,

The storms of life always come unexpectedly. You use trials to shape character and draw us closer to You because You are our shelter. Someone reading this has faced many storms in life. Wounds inflicted due to grief, divorce, abuse, etc. Pain never feels good. Lord, I ask that You cover the person who, while reading, is either in a dry season or getting ready to go into one. In the shelter of the almighty, they can find rest for their souls. Refresh them with the Word, the Living Word. Increase their strength to withstand temptation and trust in You. Thank You that after the storm comes a rainbow, symbolizing the promises You have made over their lives. Bring them peace that surpasses all understanding. Let Your Will be done. In Jesus Name, Amen.

You lived Where?

Traveling with grace we didn't know existed, stopping along the route of Omaha, Nebraska, after Hurricane Katrina, we met an eruption of depression, despair, and destruction. Leaning into our own understanding that a God I couldn't see would miraculously help us through a trying time wasn't in the forefront of my mind. However, as I traversed through my journey, the song by Mary Mary, "In the Morning," ensured me that a shift in my life would occur. Obstacles were certainly thrown into the middle, pricking at my darkened heart, convincing it that hurt and anger was a much better response than to dig into that inkling and search for truth.

While transitioning to this new chapter in my life, it never occurred to me that God would be the help that I needed and the shoulder to lean on. I was lost, broken, and confused about my life. The anger was slowly creeping its way into my heart, and I didn't know how to fight it. Where was God when I needed Him the most? I had so many unanswered questions especially experiencing this at such a young age. While living in Omaha, I encountered racism, experienced depression at a low point, and weight gain that still haunts me to this day. It didn't feel like a new beginning for me as I now lived in Omaha. I was tired of the changes that didn't bring anything positive to my life. I felt alone and wasn't sure who to call on in my misery.

Although the abuse had stopped, my mom was so far gone in her illness that we didn't even spend time with her. She was withdrawn, or maybe I was, and that's the reason why it felt this way. At times, I would escape what I was experiencing through Gospel music. Although I wasn't fully plugged into God's Spirit, the music would give me hope that things would change. Mary Mary was my favorite artist at the time. I listened to them all day and all night. I couldn't even understand what was being said in their music, but somehow, my spirit knew. The hope through their music was exactly what I needed.

I was severely depressed and overweight. Each day I would sleep and eat. The pattern continued for the three years I lived in Omaha, but Mary Mary's music kept me going. It's like, although I was struggling to make sense of my circumstances, God was in the midst of my storms with me. It was my darkest moments where it seemed like if there was a God watching over me at that time, I was being well taken care of while in my storm.

I remember one night I had a dream. I was sitting in this car while a tornado was spinning all around me. Everything that was a part of me was being destroyed, but a force kept holding me down. In retrospect, through maturity, I can see that it was God showing me He would always protect despite the circumstances surrounding me. Through that small ray of hope, it seemed to stay with me because things just kept changing. Although seasons changed and my personal life seemingly didn't become much better, I always believed that one day the sunshine would appear.

Living in Omaha, I did make some friends, and my eyes were open to the reality that I was different. When we first got to Omaha, we didn't have a vehicle. My mom had somehow met someone from a Catholic Church before we moved and began bringing us there to attend services. I remember being on a flyer for needing a car and a place to stay. What made this situation a little unsettling was seeing the same picture that my family and I had just taken the day before plastered on the front of the flyer. Now don't get me wrong, my family needed these things because we came with nothing.

The thing that did bother me was the fact that we were the only black family present at this church. I was young and didn't quite understand it. It was the first and last time we went to that church. Come to think of it, we didn't see the women whose home we went where the picture came from. Going back to my experience at a Catholic Church, the youth would separate from the adults and go to the youth ministries building at some time during the service. To get there, we would have to ride a bus for about 15 mins. On the bus, no one sat next to me. I looked at each person as they got on, but they walked right past me. One particular girl just stared at me as she walked by. I was used to being alone, so it didn't bother me that no one wanted to sit by me. When we got to the building, we talked about God for a little bit and then had prayer time. In my mind, I knew my family needed prayer, but I didn't know how it would work. I wasn't familiar with prayer and how powerful it was. It was like the first time someone had ever asked to speak on behalf of my family. It was refreshing, and I felt a little more relieved. After the prayer time, it was like the hour flew by, and we were ready to go back to the church. This time while I was on the bus, that same girl who stared at me the first time we got on the bus decided to sit next to me. She was very hesitant to sit next to me; but, I figured that she grew the courage to learn more about me.

We introduced ourselves to each other, and then she dropped a bombshell; I was the first person of color she had seen before. She went on to explain that the area she lived in was very racist and that she only saw black people on TV. She was so shocked that there were people who looked different than she did in real life. My innocence, as a child, didn't allow me to exhibit anger towards her, but instead, I graciously embraced her epiphany; and, I was excited that I just befriended someone of the opposite race. We chatted the entire time we were on the bus together. When the bus finally arrived back at the church, we said our goodbyes and went to find our parents. We never went back to that church, and I never saw that girl again; but, she left such an impression on me that I have not ever forgotten about her story.

Omaha, Nebraska, changed my life in a way that I didn't see race the same. Living in New Orleans during the early 1990s gave me a belief that Whites were the enemy. Through my young mind of not grasping the actual concept of race, I was plagued with the Civil Rights movement, and slavery as the image of my ancestors boiled a hatred in my heart for people I didn't know. Moving to Omaha brought this to the forefront as I experienced what it was like to be isolated because of my skin color. Meeting that young girl on the bus gave me a taste of racism in the Northern States.

On one occasion, my mom was called a nigger by a white man who cut her off while she was driving. It shocked me at first because I had only heard this term while watching movies in Elementary School, such as "Ruby Bridges" and "Our Friend Martin." The fact that it was 2005 and blacks were still being called niggers from whites ignited the hatred deeper within my heart. I used to hate watching interracial couples love on each other in my neighborhood. The narrowmindedness of the notion that all whites hated blacks didn't quite give me the full picture that some people allowed their heart to accept love freely from whomever loved them, despite the confinements of societal color lines. I was ignorant to the fact that interracial couples had children who in turn never asked to exist; and, I should have never been troubled by the thoughts because I didn't know any better.

Over time, the racial tensions I once experienced gradually subsided because I had the opportunity to befriend more people who were outside of my race. It opened my eyes to the reality that we were all human, and not every person of the same race was the same. Now, some may read this portion of the book and think that I'm stating we are a human race and skin color doesn't matter, but my point is totally opposite. My stance is that God created all people. We were created with the same body parts and have the same blood running through our veins. The skin complexion comes from the pigment God gave us; some stronger than others. Loving someone who doesn't share the same skin complexion as you shouldn't be so tedious. We must come to a point as a human race that we realize Love is the language we should all speak. It doesn't negate racism in our country. It, in fact, should draw us closer. Through my experience in Omaha, learning to be okay with separating my differences from another person because they have a different skin color helped me later on in life.

Ironically, God used this time for me to move to New York three years later. Now that I was open-minded to those who looked different than I did, I was prepared to meet many others and learn about their cultures as New York is a "melting pot." I encountered many other people who were Asian, European and Hispanic. I even met those who were from the Caribbean Islands, interestingly sharing the same complexion as me. I Thank God for allowing me to see the beauty in racial diversity. As I've matured, I've developed friendships with people from other countries. Though I know racism will always exist because of the spiritual warfare humans encounter on a daily basis, I'm content with the fact that God created all different shades of people to show His majesty and beauty. We all share the same blood, and it becomes more evident when we become a new creation in Christ.

Moving to Omaha sparked a change of imbalance. Here I was depressed and alone because I was away from family, but God was using this to shape my path in the near future. The music that I began to listen to changed my life. Although I wasn't ready to embrace the wisdom and knowledge of God, it inspired me to acknowledge that I wasn't alone in my everyday struggles. Finding hope in the music helped ease the pain of living uncomfortably in a place where I knew I wouldn't permanently reside and realize that eventually, there would be an ending to my current life struggles.

I was lonely at the time because my mom moved us far away from family to an unknown place where we had no family, which introduced me to a season of darkness. I didn't know anyone who lived in the neighborhood. To deal with it most of the time, I resorted to constantly eating and sleeping. Throughout some of the years of my living in Omaha, this was my method of sanity. Let me tell you: that this was one of the most miserable moments of my life. I knew that by remaining optimistic, things would get better, and misery couldn't keep me down. I began to sing the lyrics of the songs whenever I would listen to the CDs. Eventually, I started listening to other artists in the same genre, which helped me even more. I believed that God was watching over me and that my deliverance from this unhealthy environment was near. Because I believed a new change was beginning, I waited until years later to pursue my calling in such that I also would be able to follow Jesus wholeheartedly.

Upon transitioning into a new state, a year later, I found that not only was I able to hear God through music, but that going to the House of Prayer would redeem my soul and open the path to living God's purpose for my life. For three years, I dealt with depression and PTSD. We had just been uprooted from a familiar place in New Orleans to now, trying to overcome trauma in a new state. My mom was very distant at this time. She didn't really talk to us. I don't remember any pleasant moments that may have happened; I could only see the pain. She would go to her room and stay on the computer daily. She did allow us to go to school, which gave us a break from the uncomfortable environment; but, leisure time outside time wasn't frequent.

Before we left Omaha, I recall her finally limiting the freedom of allowing us to go outside often. The depression I dealt with worsened. One day I went into my mom's room to use the computer. My brother was already in there, and I caught him off guard as he abruptly closed the screen in shock. I inquired about what he was watching. Then, I asked to use the computer. To my discovery, it was "Hentai," which is anime porn. He walked out of the room, and I decided to take a look myself. That was the start of me being addicted to pornography. It gave me a high that I didn't understand. It excited me and allowed me to relieve some of the frustrations. Every day after my brother used the computer, I would secretly go in and watch "Hentai." My mom walked in on me one day, but with her illness, she didn't even register what I was doing. Several days after, a shift took place in our home.

In the blink of an eye, I thought my pain was going to finally come to an end. During this time, my mom started using the computer more frequently. I raced my brother to the computer in hopes that I could watch porn and then talk with some of my family members on Facebook.

One night, my mom told my siblings and I that we would be moving again. I was devastated. The trouble began brewing in my life again as my mom made a stunning announcement that we were going to be moving to Egypt. This was tough for me to swallow because I was just so tired of fighting battles with the new things happening to my mom. With bad news seeping in, I had a plan that I would run away from my mom again. I had it all planned that I would pack up my things and get as far away as possible from her.

The night I decided it was time to leave, things didn't end well because she somehow had a sense of my plan and chose to end it. I called the cops on her because she wouldn't allow me to leave. I was told to work it out with her and to stay put because I was way too young to venture out on my own with no family around. I instantly became numb at this point. How could a person have so much power over someone else?

After that incident, my mom pulled us out of school as "preparation" for moving to Egypt. Each day we did nothing, and I yearned for school because it was my escape. For two weeks, I hated how my life was turning out, and no one, including family, was of assistance. I figured I would come up with a plan once we arrived at the airport. My mind was racing in ways to escape from the dysfunction I was living in. In Omaha, I had no family, money, or means of returning back to New Orleans. So, I was forced to go wherever my mom was taking us. On the day of our departure, we said goodbye to Omaha, Nebraska, taking only the necessities we needed because we were traveling by car. I remember looking back at the apartment we lived in, forgetting my oversized Green Bay Packer jacket. We were not allowed to return and get it; so I had to be content with the fact that I had just left something valuable in that apartment.

Here we were on the road to New York to catch a flight to "Egypt." My mom drove the entire time, never going to a hotel in order to rest. I believe we arrived in NY in just one day. I don't remember the drive or my emotional state at the moment. At that time, I just knew that I wasn't going to be in Egypt for the rest of my life. Upon arrival in New York, I knew I would have to think of something fast. We stayed in the Howard Johnson Hotel for a day or two. I didn't think to leave at that time, and I'm sure God had made this possible. On our third day in New York, we left to go to the airport. JFK airport, where sunny skies and planes take you to new heights, is where I found myself, not metaphorically speaking. The family of five was leaving the country, with two of the occupants being forced into the unknown. Somehow, at that moment, I remembered the exact location and how far the car was from the front entrance. We had all of our bags with us and were on our way to the plane. I was slowly walking behind my mom alongside one of my brothers. My mom aggressively rushed us, but I was so filled with anger and pain that I didn't listen to her.

Taking a flight to a new country may have been the best option to embrace change without doing the heart work. This could be true in some sense; however, I was not about to leap into action in April of 2008 without some sort of direction. In a moment's notice, when I could see that my mom was many steps ahead, the adrenaline took over my body as the fight or flight response kicked in. *Run, Tanisha, Run!* My mom started to yell at me, and I paused my running for a moment as I began arguing and cursing at her. It was venom spitting at venom. My heart was ice cold, like brutal temperatures in NYC during the months of December through February.

Poisonous words were tattooed in my veins and living publicly out of my mouth. I continued to run away. Before my feet, mind and heart could get on one accord, I snapped back into reality as the tears rolled down my face while sitting in the car that brought us to this destination. I never realized that the same brother who ran away with me for Katrina was also behind me, running to the car. We both sat there, unsure of what to do next. I know for sure that God was with us because within minutes later, a woman came up behind us and told me that God told her to follow us outside. We never met this woman, and I was in total shock; but, I obviously felt a sense of ease with her embracing us. She risked her job to save my life. She was the angel God had ordained to be there for that very day.

Ordinary to the naked eye, some may think you have to be crazy to run behind two young children in one of the biggest airports in the United States; however, I call her a brave ambassador for the Kingdom of Heaven because she had no idea how that pivotal point in my life would change it forever. In light of what was taking place, the series of unfortunate events, due to unforeseen circumstances, eventually brought me dead smack in the middle of where God wanted me. The woman told us to come back inside with her as she would make sure that we were safe. My mom was nowhere in sight. When we were back inside the airport, we were escorted to the police station, which was located inside. My brother and I learned that my mom had boarded the plane with my two younger brothers, and the plane was getting ready to leave the airport. The officer was able to stop the plane and arrest my mom for neglect because she left my brother and I alone as minors. For hours the police department tried to contact my family so that we would be able to fly home. I assume they were not able to contact family members; therefore, we were taken to the hospital to examine if we had been abused or hurt.

After that night, we were taken to ACS, where things began to turn sour again. I was numb, and I decided to shut down from the outside world. I didn't want to talk or answer any of their questions. I was placed in a group home for about three days before I learned that I would be going to a new home. This was a bittersweet moment because it would be "permanent," yet my birthday was two days away, and I knew that I'd be spending it with strangers. Because of the feelings of confusion plaguing my mind, I again withdrew and shut down. The workers noticed what had occurred in me and decided it was best that I stay in the group home for another night to sleep things off.

Prayer

Father who art in Heaven,

 A sense of stability is a desire many have. We cherish the ability to stay in a place where calmness and warmth are the closest friends. Overwhelmed with doubt to shut down, I pray for those who have asked You to bring them peace. Secure in them the faith of a mustard seed to know all things work together for the believer. Hear their plea, Lord, to bring sunshine in the midst of dark clouds. The psalmist says to allow us to lay in green pastures surrounded by the waters that soothe the soul. Restore hope in moments of hopelessness, and Lord, please, give them rest to endure to the end. May You be glorified, honored and praised in Jesus Name, Amen.

The System is Rigged!

The Bible has every situation we face on a day-to-day basis. Many have said it's a book of fairy tales or a story of ancient legends. As I write my story, I always ask God to connect what I'm writing to His word. We hear that nothing is new under the sun (Ecclesiastes 1:9). The Holy Spirit revealed the life of Moses. In a short snippet, Pharaoh had sent out an order to kill any male Hebrew children under the age of two. The panic and fear that spread across the Israelites camp may be one we can never fathom. As fear settled in the land, a mom who knew the God she served could provide protection for the newborn baby boy He had just given her. Her faith had trumped fear. With tears streaming down her eyes and pain that she was faced with a tough decision, she laid that baby boy inside of a basket, covered him and believed God. The baby sailing across the River came into contact with the daughter of Pharaoh. I'm sure she knew this baby was a Hebrew, but God had softened her heart to be his caretaker. Moses, she named him. The beauty in that is that the same man who had executed the order to murder the Hebrew boys now had one in his home because of God's plan. Saints, y'all can go on ahead and shout at the revelation. Anyhow, Moses was being raised by a foster parent. Someone who was strange to him yet, God used this woman to bring glory to the purpose which would later take place when Moses had an understanding of his identity. He took on their lifestyle. A child learns what is taught to them. As we age, God gives us revelation into things if we have a willing heart towards Him. Moses received love and support from his foster mother. Though foster care looked different in those times, the same principles still applied. One is placed in someone else's care for a season. While Satan plans with the intent to kill, steal and destroy, God is the author and finisher of our faith. Moses' mom stepped out on faith, and I stepped out on faith, not knowing it existed to believe I would be okay in my next chapter.

Recounting the moment, it was my time to depart the group home and meet the woman God knew I would be placed with, the next day, I packed my things to move into my new foster home. I don't remember how long it took us to get there, but I know that when we finally arrived, I looked up into the sun shining and a house sitting pretty in the suburbs; I was in Long Island, NY. My new foster mom opened the door, and my caseworker introduced us. Once my caseworker left, it was just my foster mother and I. She seemed friendly, and her home was really nice. I didn't know how long I would be staying there or anything about foster care; but, I knew that for the moment, this would be my home. Looking around at different parts of her home while waiting for her to allow me into the room, she told my caseworker I would be staying in, and I looked at the pictures placed around. One, in particular, was of her receiving either an award or medal in a police uniform. I took a mental note of that because it was weird that she didn't mention that while introducing herself.

During my first or second day there, I don't recall what made me upset; but, I remember putting on my shoes and walking out after an argument with my foster mom. My fight or flight response was at an all-time high. On top of the fact that I was in a stranger's home, my birthday had just passed, and here I was, facing adversity. It didn't matter to me in the moment if the situation was big or small. In my mind, I had no sense of peace in the chaos forming around my life. I walked down the block, and her daughter drove up next to me. She asked if I wanted to return back to the agency. I guess she was sent out to help bring some clarity. That day I could have left her house, but I stayed because I didn't know anything about New York, nor did I want to move from place to place again.

After staying for a while, things got a little easier, and the tension eased among my foster mom and me. School had ended for kids in NY, and summer had started. I was supposed to attend summer school because I was behind in 9th grade, but with the new changes and so much transitioning going on, I couldn't attend. Due to my mom removing my siblings and I out of school before the year ended, I didn't fulfill the requirement to move onto the next grade. Although, looking at my report card, the school could have known how bright I was, no child left behind didn't apply in my case. My foster mother even mentioned before starting the regular school year that my grades were really high. I had always been an A/B student. School was my escape from the troubles I faced at home. No matter what challenges occurred, I was not going to throw my education down the drain. The website https://www.nfa.org/issues/education/, entails information about children who enter foster care that have a difficult time academically. Based upon the experience they are dealing with as a new way of life has occurred, the trauma forces them to neglect school responsibilities. The statistics on the website states, half of the youth are below average, and less than 3-4% graduate college. I can tell these were the words of the wind in these situations because my foster mom was shocked to see that my grades were strong. I was the exception to any statistics the government put out about foster children.

Though a new milestone would form in my life of repeating the 9th grade, it wouldn't change my perspective that education was my meal ticket to a better life. I had to roll with the punches and knock those statistics clean out the window. Encountering defeat with the revealed information, it didn't stop the flow of going to school. When it was time to register me into high school, I met two girls sitting outside the office. They made me feel welcomed coming into the new school. They walked up to me and asked my name and where I was from. While waiting for the registration to be complete, I chatted with the girls. It put my mind at ease to not think about repeating the grade. I didn't talk to them much for the rest of the summer, but I had a strong sense of calmness within me because I met two people who would be in the same grade as I was. Although I was excited to be in school again, repeating the 9th Grade made me feel incompetent. I was forced to take some of the same classes that I had already taken in Omaha, NE, with younger students. I was terrified at first but had to accept this fact because nothing else could be done to alter it. Two options formulated out of this truth, was I going to continue believing education was the way out or succumb to the belief of statistical facts stating that I would be a failure? I felt like my mom had once again caused an antagonizing aspect to my life due to having an episode, and I had to deal with the consequences.

As this new chapter in my life unfolded, it seemed as though my life was getting better and worse at the same time. I was finally getting what I've wanted for years: to be separated from my mom. I didn't have to run away anymore because living in the suburbs seemed to provide a healthy distraction from the turmoil I experienced being down south. While living in a neighborhood that I was unable to live in during my time in New Orleans, the green grass on the other side slapped me right in the face.

My freshman year at Roosevelt High School proved that my life was no longer going to be the same. I experienced a few rough moments during that year; but, New York, at that point, didn't turn out to be so bad. My first two years of living with my foster mother had its ups and downs, but the lows really manifested during my senior year. Before moving into the final year of my high school chapter, the sophomore through junior year, I can recount the moment God revealed Himself to me in a way I would know He existed but not to the full extent where I was ready to have a relationship with Him.

Sophomore year of high school was a turning point in my life. Fortunately, I made new friends the prior year, and things were looking a little brighter. Three friends, I met in particular, attended the same church I did. One day they invited me to attend a "Church Without Walls" event. I said yes because it was something new, and of course, I was a professing "Christian." "Church Without Walls" was an extended summer event consisting of several Gospel artists performing at Pastor Donnie McClurkin's church. It was an amazing summer for me because I was finally able to see Mary Mary perform live. It reminded me of the times I listened to their music in Omaha, Nebraska, when I was going through a depressive state. I wasn't able to speak with them face to face, but I was excited to have at least see them perform.

A few weeks later, one of my friends invited me to the church for an actual service. We attended with her aunt. I was a little hesitant for various reasons, but I wanted to be there because I desired to know more about the God I heard about in gospel music. I wanted to have a Christian lifestyle, something that was way better than the life I knew of before coming to New York. The church was foreign to me because I had a mom who didn't believe in the church. It also reminded me of how my mom tried to force my brother and I to read the Bible without fully understanding it. Not really aware that this was actually God's plan, this friend was helping me get on a path with God that I so desperately needed.

Perfecting Faith Church in Freeport, New York, was my first step to learning who Jesus was and the mission that He set for us. Finally developing enough courage to go up to the altar, as I had been attending the church for some time, I remembered surrendering to Christ for the first time as tears rolled down my cheeks and the walls of my heart came down. What I experienced prior was then coming to a complete end—at least in my mind at the time. I remembered the woman who touched my heart, praying over me and letting me know that Jesus loved me very much. What made this day even more life-changing was the after prayer and surrendering that I experienced. Pastor Donnie McClurkin said to me, "now that you have been saved, go and tell someone older than you that this has happened." I was so overwhelmed with joy that I could only think of the woman whom I lived with at the time to share the good news.

When I arrived home that day, I told my foster mother what had happened; and, instead of her showing the same excitement I did, she actually brushed it off. At the moment, I didn't understand, but now that I'm older, I know that since I made that decision and God's hedge of protection was over me, it completely contradicted her actions towards me that impacted me mentally and emotionally. The enemy manifested himself very heavily in the life of this woman, and now that I had surrendered my life to Christ, I became a threat to her. God may not have opened up my eyes at that very moment, but I can look back and see that with writing this book, I needed to go through those trials and tribulations to become who I am today.

Due to the fact that I connected with God on some level, my foster mom, whom I started calling "Auntie," appeared darker to me. Living in her home really allowed me to see her for who she was. I started to be attacked over a period of time just living with her. The verbal abuse and constant comparison of herself to God caused me to become very confused. It was as if the person I knew before no longer existed. I would constantly hear her boasting about the money she had, a brand-new Mercedes Benz, and a nice home. She would even brag about her daughter, who was the apple of her eye. I was heartbroken because I felt pressured to decide whether to choose her or God. I was staying in her home, but the trials were becoming more intense. I felt smothered. She was constantly telling me that I needed to lose weight and judged me for the types of food I liked to eat. I remember dealing with insults from the kids that lived there. They told me to go on Nutri-system or on a diet so I could lose weight. She allowed the kids to say things to me without reprimanding them. I didn't mind the weight loss goals because I really needed to get my weight back to normal. I even started walking and adopting better eating habits; however, what did hurt for sure is when I asked her one day if I was beautiful, and she replied, "you're alright, not a bad-looking kid."

Her words shattered me from that moment on. This impacted my self-esteem more than it was before. Her words still sting, and while I'm trying to repair my self-esteem on a daily basis, I'm sometimes reminded of the awful words that she said to me. Over time, I began to think I wasn't pretty enough, and that's why guys didn't ask me out on dates or try to be my boyfriend. I was isolated once again, forced to deal with negative thoughts. Even though I was away from my mom during these times, when I would see her, she would always tell me I'm beautiful and that she loved me. I couldn't understand why my mom's words weren't sinking in, but this woman I had only known a short time had more power over my emotions.

For the next year or so, I had to find the strength and courage to not allow this woman to break me down emotionally, mentally, and physically, while preparing for the time when my existence no longer would only fulfil her selfish needs. I thank God for helping me find ways to lose weight and have time away from her periodically. I decided to try out for the basketball team. I lost a lot of weight playing basketball and my self-esteem began to blossom. I had teammates who became friends, and I had a place where I could be myself. Basketball was also a stress reliever. After the season was over, I started working because working was a requirement while living there. She would tell us, "if you live in this house, you're either working or going to school." And when she contradicted herself, which was often, it was "you need a job while in school because the agency doesn't pay me enough for you." I started to get frustrated over the years with her bull crap, but God again had given me an outlet to being away from during the day.

I picked up a pattern of taking the night shifts because I had school during the day. It felt good being away from the drama. I would literally come home every day at 12am and then go to school in the morning. This was something I did until the basketball season started again in my junior year. Staying in on the weekends, though, gave me the opportunity to just show how much control she had over my emotions. I would hear her stomping down the stairs to turn on the lights and telling us to wake up because we weren't going to be sleeping in her house all day while she was wide awake. It seemed like a game to her. I honestly could have joined the military after dealing with her because she was indeed the true Master Sergeant. I tried to find plans for each weekend; sometimes it worked, and other times, I just had to deal with her for the weekend.

Going to service on Sundays was my anchor of hope. I escaped her misery for a couple of hours. I remember asking her if I could take one of the boys from home with me to church. Some days she would say yes; but, sometimes, I didn't bother to press the issue about it because I needed the space. I eventually learned that she believed I was having sex with this 12-year-old child. I mean, who in their right mind as an older teenager would bring a kid to church just to have sex with them? Or, for the matter, want to have sex with a 12-year-old? Now I know in society we see this often where older people are interested in children. I was not one of those people and still am not to this day. I honestly didn't understand it, but eventually, he stopped going to church with me. I believed that because I was able to escape from her controlling moments on Sundays, I could just be myself. That was far from the truth. She began controlling that aspect of my life as well.

I remember walking home from church one day. She spotted me coming walking down the street as I had just come from McDonalds. She told me to get in the car and then began an interrogation of asking me did I go and did I eat already. I said, "yes, of course," but, in her mind, she needed to control when I ate and what I ate. It became very draining. I was getting tired of this yet couldn't shake her because I was used to toxic people being in my life, and I was sure that I didn't want to go back to my mom. Either I had to continue dealing with her antics or make a move. Whatever the decision was, it needed to be made swiftly. My emotional sanity was becoming a cost.

Junior year was the perfect timing for a turning point to occur in my life. My senior year was approaching, and graduating high school on my way to college was my tunnel vision. I was still on the basketball team and working at one of my jobs. This job I had, in particular, was fun because the closing crew became my friends. We spent a lot of time together. When we all had the same days off, we went out to malls or movies. This was another way for me to get away with a much-needed break. I could count on these friends to have my back. It was like a breath of fresh air all in one.

I began making my own money at 16 years of age. I used it to hang out and buy my own food so that I didn't have to hear negativity from Auntie about my food choices, but she didn't let me just enjoy my money. Every paycheck, I had to bring money upstairs to her so that it could go into "savings." I would go up there so often to the point where I just stopped putting my money in there. I had to have some type of control over my life. Auntie's controlling ways really took a hit while I was working. One day, while I was on the clock, Auntie decided she would come to my register and check out items. Unbeknownst to the both of us, they had an undercover security agent upfront. She thought that she was smart by passing items and bagging them up. I was so scared of her that my mind wasn't focused on the fact that I was helping her steal food. The security guard caught wind of what was going on, and he went to my manager to let them know what had happened.

As my foster mother walked out of the store with the stolen items, my register was being closed and I was escorted to the back. Once in the office, I knew that trouble was brewing. My supervisor was so disappointed in me because we had developed a very strong relationship, and she knew I wasn't the type of person to do something like this normally. My foster mother tried to run, but they caught her and brought her back inside. The cops were called, and she tried to leave me there alone to take all the blame for what had taken place. I guess she had a "change of heart" because moments later, she reappeared into the store and in the office where I was. When the cops arrived, she insisted that they just take her only since it was her fault that the stealing occurred. The store manager thought otherwise and wanted both of us arrested. The cops looked at me, and I could sense that they knew I was just doing what I was told as a minor. The day before that happened, one of my foster sisters had just gotten fired for stealing. I never put two and two together, but somehow my time had come because Auntie had done the same thing.

Ashamed and embarrassed, I walked out of my real first job in handcuffs and was fired. I was only 16 years old. We didn't sit in the same car, and I thanked God because I could only imagine what the conversation would have looked like. I sat in the back of a cop car so ashamed of what I had done. I couldn't believe that I allowed this woman to bring my life down so low. The cops seemed pretty nice. They asked me if it was my first offense. I told them, yes, and they mentioned that I probably wouldn't be doing any time. Being pulled out of a police car and put in a jail cell is not an easy thing to process. They placed us both in the same cell. The cop began to ask our names. I learned that Auntie had a past with the law, and she didn't hesitate to tell them that she was a former police officer. The stuff that the cop brought up was from her teenage years. I was in disbelief; I was literally sitting in a jail cell with a professional criminal.

The remembrance of the moment I saw her picture with a cop uniform my first day appeared in my head. She had known the law because she practiced it for years. The government makes it clear to us that cops are there to "protect and serve." This woman knew how to manipulate situations as well as control the environment. Though she was retired, I'm told that a cop is always a cop. It was her duty to "protect and serve" instead of encouraging me to steal. My weakness had been exploited. I think besides the fact it was my first offense, we got a slap on the wrist and a class to take because she was a former police officer. Injustice had been done as I had to pick up the consequences of my actions due to the actions of someone else. I knew it was wrong to steal, but the emotional and mental damage that had been drilled in my head from one who knew how to interrogate, placed heavy fear that I should never be on her "bad" side. Living with a cop was hell. Tactics passed down in training on how to break someone's soul so that they can emulate your image has to be some sort of joke. The fear I felt for flesh created by God should have been fear for God instead. I didn't know how to stand up for myself. She knew that I was broken on the inside. Using my family against me by telling foster children all the time that if your family really loved you, then you wouldn't be in foster care. To an outsider, they would have probably agreed. What family allows their child to be taken away and placed in the home of strangers? At this point, she wasn't a stranger anymore, but she had manipulated me to get what she wanted. Again, as I realized these were tactics of police officers, I couldn't help but think that the system is rigged. I so desperately wanted out but didn't know who I could call on. Sitting in a jail cell for the first time wouldn't ease my pain.

Her "precious" daughter came to pick us up. Her daughter laughed hysterically, claiming that she couldn't believe she had to pick us both up from jail. Processing the fact that I was inside of a jail cell for the first time and had just lost my first real job didn't seem funny. I was hurt all over again but stayed because it was the "right" thing to do. This woman had brainwashed me into believing in her lies, and due to my emotional weakness, I fell for it. Though she was giving me a new life, I understood that those in the upper-middle class had their own struggles. She was living a lie and used her "love" for children to cover it up. To make matters worse, she had no empathy for what had occurred. The next day, she told me I needed to find a new job. I was so numb to her mental and emotional abuse, that I went along with it. She was an adult and knew better than me. I had to obey.

Sticks and stones may break my bones, but words don't hurt me. How many of you have heard that saying growing up? What a lie from the enemy. Being in denial at the fact words hurt, have caused so many to bottle up emotions and masquerade behind a smile. Trapped in the home of a woman I thought could "save" me from my troubles came as a rude awakening. Her words, her actions dampened my spirit. I was crushed on the inside. No one came to soothe my wounds. They festered until I encountered Jesus. When I realized that coming home late was more peaceful than sitting and looking in her face all day, I knew it would only be a matter of time before I left. I had a habit of running away from my problems. It wasn't the ideal way to process trauma but fight or flight was the testimony I had at the moment. I couldn't look in the mirror and smile at the reflection I saw. I didn't believe I was beautiful. God creating me wasn't a mistake; the features He had given me reflected His majesty. The beauty possessed in a being from a beautiful designer. Due to not really having a heart of flesh, Auntie could only express what was on the inside of her heart; that happened to be darkness. Ugly things breathe within the dark waters. Hiding behind shadows, the enemy used her to damage me, believing I would never have faith in Christ or see myself the way He intended. It is his job to make me lose my faith before establishing a true relationship with the Father. Oftentimes, we have no idea how God will use a vessel. I, for one, just figured going to church was enough, setting me up for failure because I lack wisdom on how to pursue God. Satan thrives in ignorance. The biggest lie he has convinced the world to believe is that he doesn't exist. Deep in our minds, whether we acknowledge it or not, we know that God exists. Satan has blinded humans with the problems we face at the hands of each other. The saying, "throw a rock and hide your hand," has his name written all over it. Auntie had the Bible opened on a nightstand in the hallway before entering her bedroom. She knew of God but somehow had lost her way. She thrived in making children believe she set the standard for beauty.

Living in darkness deceives one if we are not planted on good soil. The enemy had deceived us both. Yet, God, in His infinite wisdom, has destroyed the plot of the enemy over my life. I have been redeemed through the blood of the Lamb. No matter what she said or did, it didn't stop the plan to come to know Jesus for myself. I rest in the fact that encountering her when I did was necessary. Shifting my energy to something else was one way to help dissolve some of my thoughts. The rest of my junior year was a blur; I had to focus on my senior year because the journey ahead required me to be aware of what was going on.

Senior year was like a breath of fresh air, although I was still living with my foster mom and dealing with so many other things. The time was getting closer for me finally going away and doing something more important with myself. A college setting sounded so much more relaxing, as like many of my peers thought it would be like the colleges in movies and TV. I was prepared for a lot of college friends, parties, meeting my soulmate, and having the most awesome experience that occurred once in a lifetime. I had no idea that I would again have to face the enemy's attacks in which my freshman year of college would become a living nightmare.

Before I could officially embrace the next portion of my life, I had to get through my senior year. I had stopped playing basketball, but now, I was a part-time cashier at Wendy's. I picked up a pattern again of taking the night shift and coming home late just to be up in a couple of hours for school. Some days, I was really tired, but powering through as opposed to dealing with her antics was worth it. Looking ahead to what senior year included was my light in the darkness.

I started working with the Education Specialist at the Foster Agency I was a part of. She knew what I was going through in this home because she herself had been through the foster care system. She explained the process I would be going through and to be sure of the choice I wanted to make for college. Senior Year was coming to a close. I was awarded scholarships both from the agency and school. Things were looking up, and I was ecstatic about my future. I sent out my college applications and applied for maybe 1-2 scholarships outside of the ones I had received. Two of the colleges accepted me, Howard University and St. John's University.

Prayer

Lord God Almighty!

    You are the One who sits on the throne. You sit high and look low. I thank You that we have a mediator between man and God. Lord, I pray for the person who has been in the foster care system. Every season we experience is to strengthen our faith and bring glory to Your Name. To the person in the foster care system now, I pray that You would cover them under the shadow of Your wings. Lead them to people whose foundation is set on Your Word. Show them that You are real and that You love them deeper than the oceans. We don't have to succumb to any number or plot the enemy has used to try and destroy us. Lead them to the place where the light shines brightly. I pray for the restoration of joy and peace in their hearts. To the parents: please give your child grace if God returns them to you. Jesus, I thank You for bringing me to a place where I can be open to the possibility that healing is always there for the broken-hearted. May You be glorified, honored, and praised in Jesus Name, Amen.

The System is Rigged!

Unforeseen

I can remember since the age of 10, a few mishaps would occur around the time of my birthday. Some of those mishaps outweighed the good, but I can't say that every birthday was terrible. In the year 2012, as my senior year approached its end, I began the process of sending out applications for college. Some of them had fee waivers which was a high schooler's dream; most cost money students didn't have. One of the schools was St. John's University. I just applied to it with no intentions of attending. The other two were for Stonybrook and Howard University. I didn't receive a fee waiver for those, but I applied anyway because of their reputation. During the end of the year, I was staying with a friend. I had gotten into a verbal altercation with Auntie and decided to "run away." My friend's mom allowed me to stay there until things cooled off. I just so happened to be at my friend's home the day of my birthday. I received my first application update; it was a rejection letter from Stonybrook. I actually was interested in attending Stonybrook because I had visited the campus during a college tour planned by the high school. The rejection kinda put a little discouragement in my heart, but I didn't allow it to bother me as much. Within an hour or so, I received an email from St. John's University. At first, I was a little nervous because of what happened with Stonybrook, but when I opened the email from St. John's, I received an acceptance letter. My birthday had turned around. A few days later, I was accepted to Howard University. Howard University was placed at the top of my list because I wanted to attend an HBCU. I was determined to go as I heard so many great people attended Howard, and one of my favorite teachers graduated from there. I had it set in my heart that Howard University was going to be my Alma Mater. I could imagine myself there meeting some chocolate cutie who would become the love of my life. My teacher had given us some insight into meeting the "college cuties." She told us there were 31 flavors of men there; so we had better be careful. We would enjoy college because it was such an experience. I was full of excitement; this new experience was what I had to have after dealing with another layer of trauma. I envisioned college to be exactly what I saw on TV. The easiest classes, hot professors, and parties all day, all night. I didn't know that the temptations of the world were in full throttle when you entered a college campus. It was the American Dream; It would end in reward of a high-paying job and a good look on your resume. I thought about that over and over again as the time got closer. With my hopes up high, I experienced a heavy crumbling down moment when my foster mother learned of my choice.

My decision to attend Howard University was shot down as my foster mother decided to step in because she always had to have her input. She told the Education Specialist who was helping me that I should stay and attend St. John's because of my medical condition. She was using my own traumatic situation against me. Because I was vulnerable and still lived with her, I changed my mind. I told the Education Specialist that my choice was now to attend St. John's.

I couldn't even be angry with what she had done because I really feared this woman. She knew that I wouldn't dare try to step on her toes, so her saying this to the Education Specialist in front of me was a landslide. I didn't want to attend St. John's University. Why was it that she had so much influence over my mind and heart? I just knew that attending an HBCU would be where I would thrive, especially being around people who looked like me. This was supposed to be my choice, yet I forfeited it to please someone else. There was never a time to stand up to her. I didn't fight often because I knew fighting wasn't a problem solver. I walked out of the agency with a coerced last-minute decision.

The Education Specialist grew suspicious. She asked me if I was really sure that this was the decision I wanted to make or if I was pressured into it. I went ahead and lied, telling her St. John's was going to be my choice. Auntie not only used my life tragedy as a con way to keep money flowing to her, but she was also showing the control she had over me once again. Succumbing to the pressure dampened my desire for college for a while. The excitement I had before simmered down as I had to deal with the impact of yet another attempt to steal my joy from the hands of my foster mother. I began to think that I was going to be able to stay with my friend for the time being and that once I entered college, things would be different. That situation was halted when my friend's mom discussed with me that I should go back to live with my foster mom. I told her okay even though I wasn't ready. She decided to drop me off there, and as I got out of the car, I saw Auntie handing her some money. What a tragedy to see that I had a price put on my head for my friend's mom to "hush" instead of letting the agency know what had taken place. I was disgusted. I never mentioned to my friend what occurred between her mom and Auntie; I just kept that secret to myself for years. Auntie had won the game once again, even in her persuasion to make sure a paycheck continued coming to her home; the same paycheck she swore wasn't enough to take care of me.

Even though she used manipulation to keep me under her thumb, I was really excited because college was a new beginning for me. I finally mustered up the strength to see the bright side of what took place. I set in my mind that she was not going to steal the show completely. College was still the best choice I made for my future, and it was just going to be fulfilled at St. John's University.

Now that I made a new decision, it was time to get equipped for the next chapter in my life. I wanted to know what was in store for me, and I was ready to embrace a college kid mindset. My preparation was simple: find out who my roommates are, buy all the necessary things I would need to stay there, and just enjoy the rest of the summer until it was time to move in. St. John's had sent out a newsletter with the things that we would need, and since I had the majority of the supplies on the list, I was prepared to move in on the designated date. Before I moved into my dorm room, plans were getting unfolded, which would allow me to go on and start fresh away from Auntie.

During that period in the summer, before moving into the dorms, I visited my relatives in Louisiana. I had just recently started going back there after 4 or 5 years, and I was always happy to be back in the lives of my extended family. I was enjoying myself to the fullest and had no knowledge that my foster mom had another agenda. This woman never stopped. It was always something else. I don't know how I stayed with her all those years, but I did. While in New Orleans, I received a text message from her daughter letting me know that I should stay with my mom for a few days because Auntie wasn't home. I knew that it was a lie because she had used those very same words to a bill collector while she was sitting at the edge of her bed. With frustration and anger beginning to seep in, that night I had made up my mind that I would no longer be returning to her home. I finally became fed up with the antics. I grew more courageous, and I didn't have to tolerate disrespect from anyone even if they opened up their home to me for a season. The breaking point had gotten where it needed to be for me to move forward.

I came back to New York with different intentions and went straight to my mom's. My summer was well spent after that, and I was prepared to start this new life as a college student. I returned to my mom's house and asked her if it was okay to stay in her home until I moved on campus. She was happy that I shared the news with her. I literally called Auntie the next day and asked her to bring all of my things because I wouldn't be returning to her home. I could sense the shock through the phone. In my mind, explaining to her what I was feeling couldn't compare to the peace I experienced, telling her that I had enough. Even though those weren't my exact words I used to send the message. I'm not sure what time she came, but my brother answered the door, and while I sat there, he told her I wasn't home. My brother grabbed all of my things from her. That day, in August of 2012, I walked away from Auntie and never spoke to or saw her again.

It has been eight years, and sometimes I want to stop by to tell her how great my life has become since I found Jesus, but my anxiety has never allowed me to. For me, this is God's way of telling me to leave that chapter closed and continue to move forward. If this book ever lands in her hand, I would be humbled to let her know that she is forgiven and God has made me new.

Prayer

Father who art in Heaven!

This prayer is for the person who has seen the dark side of being in foster care. With a shattered heart caused through pain that left them in the hands of a stranger, I pray for full healing in Jesus Name. Open up the heart of this person to trust in You more. Lead them to the way that's everlasting; a promise to those who diligently seek You. I pray that this person would feel Your Love that is abounding. The vengeance is Yours to take, and they can rest in the fact that You take care of those You call Your children. I thank You for being a Father to the fatherless and motherless. You restore beauty for ashes. May You be glorified, honored and praised for this beautiful soul in Jesus Name, Amen.

Girls Gone Wild!

While attending Perfecting Faith Church, my friend I had been attending with for a while, came up to me after service one day to let me know that God sent a message through a woman to my friend to relay to me that I had a calling placed upon my life. Hearing those words for the first time didn't fully register. For one, I didn't know what a "calling" was or what God had in store. I shrugged off what my friend had told me and went about the rest of my day. I never saw that friend again. Connections had been lost because I moved away from Long Island, and I wanted to separate myself from anything that would remind me of my time spent there. Losing friendships was okay with me at that point, a "fresh start" was my motto. I pushed for it, and it landed right in my lap.

College is what I called the beginning stages of adulthood and reality. It was like four years of high school put into one. I had high expectations going into college based upon what I was told from my teachers. Knowing that I was finally away from Auntie and now my mom again gave me the sanity I needed to start new. No longer connected to the past, I was about to rediscover myself and learn how to manage my trauma while understanding my identity. I was in for an unexpected challenge. Adapting was going to get me to the next level; but, first I had to encounter the challenges head-on.

Ah, freshman year, you were now in full effect. In August of 2012, following that surprise email, I moved into my new dorm room on St. John's campus. I was the last one that day to arrive in the room because my mom and I encountered some delays. Once I arrived, I knew that it would be different for me because my roommates and one of my suitemates had already formed a clique which is not something

I'm used to or fond of. I also felt very awkward, as if I didn't quite belong there. The tension had already started. As each suitemate moved in, I tried to engage in conversation to become acquainted with them and see who I would get along with. I wanted to get along with them because I would be living with seven other girls alone in a college dorm for the entire year. This was something I was going to have to suck up in order to survive what is now known as one of my many tests. I was used to it though, because, during my time living in my old foster home, I always shared a room with two or three girls.

Throughout that time in the suite (Bad Girls' Club, as my roommate named it), the experience was quite interesting. I experienced some tension and awkwardness during my first meeting with the girls; the gut feeling was starting to come alive. My second week is what made me know that this year was going to be a time to remember. One of my roommates had a birthday coming up, and being the kind-hearted person I was, I planned to do something nice for her. I was always very friendly and yearned for people to like me. I learned later that this is called codependency.

Anyway, I liked to cook and figured I would make the whole suite breakfast as a celebration. That decision turned into a major disaster. We had fire drills to help us be prepared in the event that something would happen because we had a kitchen on one of the floors. I was prepared to go in to cook the food and surprise my roommate with breakfast and an Oreo ice cream cake, which was her favorite. As I got up early that morning, while everyone slept, I made my way to the kitchen. I was going to cook bacon in the oven and make eggs and waffles. I didn't have a pan, so I put the bacon on aluminum foil in hopes that it wouldn't burn. I had forgotten that you're supposed to fold the foil to make it look like a mini pan. I learned firsthand as I placed the bacon on to let it cook while I toasted the waffles. While cooking, I begin to smell the bacon burning. I looked in the oven and saw the bacon fat dripping down onto the actual oven. As the oil started to burn, it got even worse. The fire alarm went off. It was 8 or

9am something in the morning, and the whole entire building had to evacuate.

To say people were pissed was an understatement. I told my roommates when we all got outside that I was trying to cook us breakfast, and they walked away from me in anger. The fire department was called, and they put out everything. I didn't set the building on fire (Thank God); but, I was really hurt because my roommates didn't eat the food that was cooked, everyone was upset because they were awakened out of their sleep, and my birthday idea was ruined.

The girls who had formed the clique left and went to breakfast instead at the dining hall, and the cake that I bought was thrown out. She didn't even eat it after I gave it to her. With a face flood of tears, I went to my RA at the time to tell her that I was the one that set it off. She made me feel a lot better as she explained that her freshman year was rough as well because she set her bed on fire. I honestly thank God for the RA I had freshman year, even though we had some downtimes. She helped me cope with many things, and she also became a good friend.

That incident and a chain of other events caused my room to be the "Bad Girls' Club." We were living that nightmare, picking sides and making others feel like an outcast. Having to live in a room with two other girls who didn't understand me felt very isolating. Throughout my year in that room, I had to separate myself because most of the girls' focus was on boys, High School friends they had, and conjuring a lot of drama that I really didn't want to be a part of.

In High School, I was one of those people who knew everyone but didn't have a certain group to hang out with all the time. That was something like the girls on TV, and I wanted to be a friend to everyone in each group like I did when I was in High School. As I mentioned before, prior to going to college, I had been told that college was where you find your lifetime friends, discover your soulmate, and party a lot. I believed for the moment that these girls and a few other people, whom I had met, would be those lifetime friends that I would share college stories and fun times with in college.

For me, that should have been the last thing I had to worry about because it opened my eyes to the reality of the world and the reality that if I had not found Jesus in the midst of it all, I was going to sink. I was being spiritually attacked often by my roommates. They would go out with each other and didn't tell me. I was embarrassed, and I didn't want to go back home because I had spent so many years trying to avoid it. One day, they decided I could be a part of their clique. We linked up to go to Times Square in Manhattan. I was excited because, seemingly for the first time, we were all getting along. Things were going well until we got lost going back to campus. I was the only one from New York at the time, but I didn't really know too much about the train system. Due to this mishap, I went the only way I knew how to get to St. Johns. My roommates were furious with me. I shut down because of how I was feeling and moved away from them.

They followed behind, yelling at me. Because I had shut down, I couldn't hear or see them. My fight or flight response had kicked in. We were on the bus, and I couldn't believe what just happened. The hurt crept in again. My mom's house became clear as the only "safety net" to get back to St. Johns. I got off the bus and completely walked away from my roommates. I went to my mom's house and explained what took place. I couldn't articulate my words because of the pain I was feeling on the inside. I understood the part I played in this later on, but at that moment, I could only see how it was affecting me.

I went back to the dorm where all the girls had found their way to. I walked in silently, not saying a word to anyone. I shut down for the week. I didn't know what to say or how to say it; this was not going the way I had planned. I made a mistake that day, and the lesson I should have learned from the breakfast incident hadn't resonated with my spirit just yet. At no point in my freshman year did things get better.

I tried often to be friends with all who lived in the dorm room with me, but my past had set the tone and the present wasn't hopeful. I ended my freshman year in another dorm room. Two of the girls had moved out already; both to immature behavior and personal reasons. Them leaving brought my suitemates and I a little closer; but, my roommate and I just couldn't see eye to eye. We came to an end before the semester was over. I learned that my roommate was using Twitter to cyberbully me. Each time her friends from campus came around, I would hear snickers and get side-eyes. I wasn't sure about it until one day, one of my friends that I met at St. John's told me that my roommate had been putting things about me on Twitter. I made a fake account and followed her to see if it was true.

I was stunned. She was playing her role well. It was like I could see her for who she truly was on Twitter. I went to my RA to show her what my roommate wrote on Twitter. To both of our surprise, my roommate had written things about my RA as well. We took screenshots of the tweets, and my RA was able to bring it to the head of the schools. I wasn't sure of the disciplinary actions my roommate received, but she was very unhappy. She began to do little sneaky things like sigh when I walked into the room or leave when I came in. It came to a point where we both were very uncomfortable in one another's presence. Her petty antics continued to the last straw. I had moved to the empty bed in the room because my other roommate had moved back home. I didn't have to sleep on the top bunk anymore. It was annoying having to climb up there every day and sometimes do it silently when I came in very late because both of them were sleeping.

The roommate who lived in the room as me chose to be really petty one day. I came back from hanging out with my friends to my bed being on the bottom bunk; she had moved it. I immediately went to my RA about it instead of arguing with her. My RA put in a request for me to move out. I was upset because I didn't understand how my roommate could continue to do what she did, and I had to leave. I just took the answer and ended up moving out because the breaking points had been reached. I ended my freshman year inside a dorm room where I was uncomfortable. Moving into an established room was hard. I didn't talk with any of the girls, and I really felt out of place at this time. I did get to meet some cool people, most of whom I smoked with. I learned that each step in life has its challenges, and if not careful, you can drown in your own thoughts/subconscious. It sucked because I was so ecstatic about this new journey I embarked on, I envisioned it to be much different. Once again, I was ready to move on to the next chapter.

Prayer

—⚡—

Heavenly Father,

In Your Word, You have called us friends. When the foundation of the world was established, before creating man, You said, "Let us make man in our own image." The image describes unity before we were on the scene. You have always been about human connection, reflecting the relationship between the Trinity. Friends are necessary just as strongly as family. For those who have desired Godly friendships or have had issues with friendships in the past, this prayer is for them. I pray for those who have gone through tumultuous relationships resulting in the severity of ties with one they called friends. I pray for their heart and mind to be at peace with the Holy Spirit. Bring them comfort, Lord, to know that You are always near and is a friend that can be trusted with all things. All in all, let You be glorified through it. In Jesus Name, Amen.

Series of Unfortunate Events

During my freshman year, I picked up the habit of smoking weed. It allowed me to escape what I was dealing with in my dorm room before I moved out. I had made a vow in high school that I would never smoke weed, and here I was doing the exact opposite. I had gone to my mom's house one weekend to just visit her and my brother. I told my mom that I was about to start smoking weed. She, at the time, was a weed smoker, so she told my brother and I that she should be the first person we should smoke with. That night, I took my first puff. We smoked together, and then I said my good-byes to them. I was hooked; it brought me out of my reality and into this fantasy world. Getting high was my addiction.

I began to smoke on a daily basis: sometimes 2-3 times a day. It gave me a chance to go into another world and forget about the pain I was facing. Smoking brought me new friendships. It's like once you start, you tend to find out who all the potheads are. At one point, I smoked with one of my roommates. It became a pattern of destruction. I would say weed is all you need. My addiction eventually led my grades to plummet. Between the drama that was unfolding in my dorm, to dealing with trauma, grades getting low and my addiction growing; it became evident that I needed an intervention. Who could I run to? I wasn't thinking of God at this time because weed was my new god. I moved out of the dorm room from my roommates and still had residue from foster care.

Misery was compelling, yet somehow, I was still standing my freshman year. After the chain of events that occurred, I cried because it was so overwhelming. On top of dealing with the girls in my room, I was also still dealing with the agency. The agency told me my senior year of High School that they would be helping me pay for school as long as I kept going to school. To my knowledge, I thought that meant that things were going to be easy, and I would be going to school for free. This was true, but there were consequences, or should I say so much more than handing in info about your school, and they would help you pay. There was a process that needed to take place every semester before they released funds. Any person who has gone to college knows dealing with finances of any sort is excruciating. In the midst of dealing with the agency, I was still dealing with my roommates. I decided that getting a job of some sort would be smart so that I could at least take care of myself while the agency helped pay for college. I had to get a job because I quit my old job from High School to focus more on college.

Sorting out finances and having to go through a process with the agency took a toll on my emotional state. I was tired of having to deal with them and wanted to sever ties, but I needed them in order to stay afloat for school. Living on campus was the best option for me, in my personal opinion, because I just wasn't ready to stay with my mom again. Making plans with the agency to pay for school helped push me to know that I would be fine on school grounds. Though the agency was going to pay for all of it, they always took their time with it, which didn't help the policy of St. John's. Colleges want their money at a certain time, so I often grew impatient with the agency because I didn't get why it required so much to help someone; they told me they would be getting the help.

My campus living almost came to a close. It was St. John's that stated that the bill must be paid in order for me to move back into my dorm. I started dealing with their BS more now because the agency wanted so many documents from the school from a state regulation that told them that they didn't provide this information to outsiders. The agency would make late payments, and at one point, they told me to look for outside housing so that they could afford it. I didn't know it would be a big deal, but she explained to me that my school was expensive because it's private and Catholic; but, she never said it to me when we were discussing my decision to attend St. John's. I was given a rough time again with the agency because fall semester had ended, and I had moved into a new foster home. From what I had been told, foster parents receive a monthly stipend to use for the children that lived there. The agency also delayed them and made it difficult to live with my new foster mom and school in the upcoming semester.

Upon my entrance to my new foster home, things seemed to be moving smoothly. I had met a new friend, and I was very comfortable there. The girl was a year younger than me, and she smoked weed like I did. We instantly clicked, and then I learned that our birthdays were very close to one another. Having someone who was in the same boat I was in, made dealing with another foster home much easier. We would hang out every day during the summer. I was able to meet her family and have good times. It took my mind off of my freshman year. It was like having a sister I didn't ask for.

We eventually started sharing the room. We would crack jokes and smoke each day. She was a party girl, and I just tagged along to have some freedom. Each time I had a break from school, I was allowed to come back to my new foster mom's home to stay. Having a summer breeze with a newfound friend made the transition into sophomore year something to look forward to. I always knew that I had someone to link up with if I was on vacation from school. We would go to BBQs, Parties, and I even attended her High School graduation. I loved supporting people no matter what stage of their lives I walked into.

Going back into the spring semester, I almost missed the opportunity to move in because of the agency with their late payments. Everything worked out anyway (Thank God), and I was able to move in. What started up in freshman year in regard to the payment of my room and board picked up in my sophomore year. During the summer of living at my current foster home, the school had sent in a bill that needed to be paid before I could enter into my new dorm room. I had to wait until they had cleared my payment and I could move in. I was frustrated because this was the second year in a row this was happening, and I didn't want a repeat of my freshman year. Things were still running smoothly at my current foster home as she was okay with me being there until the agency sorted things out.

Once I had finally moved in, it seemed that things were getting better. I had met a current friend my freshman year, who was also experiencing tension in her dorm room. We decided that we would become roommates, and I agreed because we were both Christian girls. Things began going smoothly in the beginning, we smoked together as well, but my friendship with her was a little different because she was a sister in Christ. Things began to change between us as she developed a relationship with her new boyfriend. I actually knew him better than she did because he and I always hung out when they weren't spending time together. I warned her that he was not good for her. I knew some stories that he shared with my former roommates and I about his past at home. My friend didn't really listen to me because she was so engulfed in him.

This warning eventually backfired on me. Although he and I were close, I didn't like who I discovered him to be after learning that he cheated on my friend multiple times, which is something I later had to discuss with her. I also despised the fact that they were having sex in the room. We had made a mutual understanding that rooming together was God's plan. We would have worship sessions and read the Word but eventually felt torn because our mutual friend was dragging her along.

I remember things turning sour one day. I went out into the common area so that I could study for tests and complete homework assignments. I knew that he had come in because we spoke before he went into the room. To get refreshed and take a break, I decided to go back into the room. I walked in on them having sex. I was so shocked that I stood there for a minute before I turned around and walked out. I became upset and had to tell her later that she should not have been having sex with him in our room, especially without warning me that they were deciding to do this. After that, I explained to her that he shouldn't be allowed in the room because it was inappropriate, especially considering the fact that she was not in the room alone.

This event caused a lot of tension in our room, which led us to stop speaking to one another. I wrote her a letter that explained why I was upset with her, but she wouldn't budge as she was so attached to the guy. She went on to tell me that I had no right to say what I did in the letter, and she, in turn, was upset as well. They decided to take their business to his room instead. I'm not sure when I told her that he cheated, but she was so intertwined with him that she still stuck with him after numerous coercions, and our relationship plummeted. I moved in with one of her friends back home, who was also one of our Christian friends.

Dealing with that situation helped me to understand that I should have chosen not to voice my opinion, but I also struggled with the thought that if we made a pact to hold one another accountable, then my letter was necessary. She and I started having arguments all the time; it was draining. Toxic communication seemed to be the only way we knew how to express ourselves. I couldn't handle this, so moving out was the best option. We tried to rebuild our friendship, but the timing wasn't in our favor.

Our arguments became a new normal. She was the first person I had ever encountered such a strong argument with. My understanding of friendship was centered around the notion of having similar interests and being mutual confidants when experiencing tough times. In all of my life, I was able to have great communication with others. I don't know if it was my lack of maturity and smoking that hindered me from communicating effectively with her, but this friendship was beginning to be too much to handle.

We stayed in this toxic friendship up until college graduation. She had finally broken up with our mutual friend, but the damage had already been done. We tried seeing eye to eye, but our personalities clashed often. I figured she was to blame because it was her lack of listening to me about the guy friend. I explained that I knew more because the conversations he had with us outside of their relationship put things in perspective. He was a complete loser. On top of that, knowing that he was fooling around with other girls that I knew of and lying about it didn't help.

She would tell me that I was too blunt and that I wouldn't be able to reach people without love. This was our issue all the time. I was trying to make her see that I had good intentions and that she was tainted by a false sense of love. Eventually, we severed our friendship. Years later, God brought to my understanding that sometimes some people can't see things the way we want them to because it's not their time to understand. I also learned that compassion was always needed in times like this. I told this to the friend after some time apart; our friendship was never restored. Now that I'm more mature in Christ, I honestly wouldn't want to deal with that type of friend again. I'm sure she has matured just as much as I had, but for some reason, our differences were stronger than our similarities. I had to move on, and so did she. The old needed to go, and new was embraced.

Prayer

Dear Lord!

It is so easy to get caught up in what is going on in others' lives that we forget to take a look at our own. This prayer is for one who has the plank in their eye. The person who sees the flaws of others yet is unable to realize that they need the Savior just as much. I pray for their mind to be renewed and washed with the blood. This prayer is not to condemn but simply to make us aware that we can deceive ourselves into believing we are more "holier" than someone else. I've learned that each person has been given a walk to fulfill the calling on their lives. I pray that they would have eyes to see and ears to hear what You are saying. Draw them closer to You, Lord, so that they may see relationship outweighs religion. Thank You for reaching this soul today! I pray that You are Glorified in Jesus Name, Amen.

Thank God for Jesus!

While sitting in my room during a break from college, God strategically placed on my heart that I would birth a book through my mishaps of trials and tribulations I experienced during the course of my time here on earth. I was afraid and unsure at first because I didn't know how this should happen and when. Through my fear and being pushed out of my comfort zone, the book weighed heavily on my heart. I knew that I would have to share this because God was going to bring some serious healing to those He purposely destined to read this book. I couldn't believe He wanted me to write my story for the world to witness, writing about how I found peace in the love of a Father I didn't know existed until I had come to a low point in my life. Instead of succumbing to my flesh and losing faith, I decided with the help of God to turn this test into a testimony with hopes that people all over the world understand how God turned my ashes into beauty.

My new beginning was becoming a new beginning. Now that I was accepting the renewal of my heart and mind plus writing this book God placed in my heart, I had to make some more changes. Here I was about to embark on an extravaganza that's so powerful and worthy because I began to trust God and knew that if this was something of His planning, I had a lot of work to do. The title begins to seep in as well because a book is not a book without a title. Through my thinking and thinking, a light bulb went off in my mind. *My Life through Christ'is*. The title was perfect and really put a deeper understanding of what it has been like since I was placed on this earth.

The prayer, "Thy Will be done on Earth as it is in Heaven," is then brought to life by God because He has timed the chosen one for their gift. Before receiving the proper correction and information on our calling, God has to transfer the gift from heaven unto earth. With the transferring, this means that God has ordered the steps in preparation for what is to come. Bishop Noel stated that "once the gift is transferred from heaven unto the earthly vessel, the recipient is now open for a direct attack from the enemy." He used Jesus as an example. Jesus came to earth as God in the flesh. To make the point clearer, he states in James 1:13, when tempted, no one should say, "God is tempting me." "For God cannot be tempted by evil, nor does He tempt anyone."

The reason for Jesus being tempted by the enemy is because He was now flesh. The enemy can't attack God, so with each gift presented to the recipient that God trusts with it, the opportunity is now open for the enemy's attack. The enemy doesn't know the intention for God's use of your gift, so the attack is then orchestrated towards you in order to prevent the gift from being used. The thing is, by the time the enemy sets up to attack, it is already too late. He goes on to further explain that this is double confirmation. In our spirits, we know that we have a gift, but what makes it so extraordinary is the attack from the enemy that lets the chosen vessel know that God has indeed gifted them and that He intends to use the gift for His purpose. Although we go through trials and tribulations because of the anointing, the result of the attack is now void because the enemy can never win.

The world sells us the idea that the secret to happiness is sex, drugs and money. At one point in my life, I believed this to be true because I would look up to celebrities and false idols who interpret themselves as "Christian" to set this standard or goal for how I should live my life. There would be days when I would think, *maybe that would be me;* but, then again, I'm reminded that I have my own goals and plans in life to glorify God, and I must not covet my neighbor's life choices or try to mimic them. The world teaches us that in order to have success, you must go to school for almost 14 years of your life, go to college afterward so that you may obtain a degree, and work tirelessly throughout your adult life until you can live without a job (retirement). These things are true to a certain extent, but just the thought of spending the rest of my time in school sounds like frustration. I will not convince anyone to leave school or any other thing for that matter unless God told you so.

This is how I felt after my second year of college, I had finally let go of what happened the year before, and things started to look up but what I didn't know was that soon I would have to, in turn, face another storm. Storms are a way of testing our faith and strengthening us to bear this cross that has been placed so that we may become Christ's disciples.

Matthew 16:24, "Whoever wants to be my disciple must deny themselves and take up their cross and follow me." What does this mean? I struggled with understanding this verse because for my 22 years here on earth, I always wanted things to go my way. Many of us can attest to this because we all, at some point, weren't on the path that God needed us to be. Before starting this journey towards fulfilling God's purpose for my life, I didn't understand that giving up everything to follow Jesus was a must. Giving up everything means stepping aside and allowing that well-known statement, "Let Jesus take the wheel," come to life. At 22, with no sense of guidance (at least not the proper way), I stood unsure as to what was required of me to become this Christ-like disciple. I chose this verse in particular because it speaks volumes, and it details the way to make possible how each of us who encounters God begins this journey of walking with Jesus.

Although it may invoke feelings of loneliness, this walk doesn't require you to be alone because the Holy Spirit guides us even though sometimes God will make known that it will be you and Him. Guidance from the Holy Spirit enables us to become Christ-like disciples, as discipleship is a form of discipline. Discipline in the sense that I struggled with it because I wasn't accustomed to going in the direction God wanted me to. His discipline breaks you out of your comfort zone and forces you to grow and be strengthened to be who

He has called you to be. I had to go through many tests and trials (as mentioned earlier) so that I could be well trained for the road to come. This road is indeed a long path (God willing) of pain and affliction. I would encourage anyone to start the journey. However, I want to acknowledge the fact that it becomes a path of pain and affliction because you are no longer choosing to conform to the world.

Before you can become a Christ-like disciple, you must know how to while understanding the purpose of Jesus carrying His cross and walking to Calvary. *The Passion of the Christ*, I would say, is a powerful movie that depicts the life of God's favor on Mary, Jesus as a young child about His Father's business, each character finding their way to Jesus so that they can be healed and their sins forgiven, but the most important, why Jesus had to endure what was necessary in order to complete the destiny that God had intended for Him while on earth. Jesus set an example of how painful it can be (through the World) to follow God and also doing God's will and not our own. I say that it is painful going through the world because to follow Jesus, you must not conform to the world. Replacing your fleshly life for a Godly life requires this because the world deceives you. Now that you have willingly given up the world and chosen to seek God's purpose for your life, the world attacks your character.

Throughout the movie, we see this happen to Jesus as every miracle He performs has backlash from the people watching (The Pharisees and Sadducees, to be specific). How often do we get confronted with outsiders who choose not to believe or even those who claim to believe in the Gospel look down upon you because of the way Jesus is teaching you? For example, I have had many heated discussions with those who chose to conform to the world because of either disbelief or not understanding what the Scriptures are saying.

Flashback: One particular time, I was in my Philosophy class, where I was told that the professor would be teaching philosophy from the perspective of an Atheist. He didn't bluntly come out and speak it, but through the philosophies of his teaching, he had his students believe that God didn't exist. My beliefs of God creating the world drove conflict because the way he twisted Scriptures and beliefs through science meant that science could answer every possible thing here on earth and that God's existence was unnecessary. I had to bring certain viewpoints to life, with love and compassion, of course, and explain to the class what the Scriptures taught.

Between constant philosophical and scientific theories, my brain got to the point of wanting to scream because it was upsetting that this is how the devil manipulates people. Not only did I have to discuss the right viewpoint with the professor, I had classmates with the same mentality as he did and science majors attacking me, telling me that I was wrong in my thinking, although at the end of the class, I was able to see God reveal Himself without the class seeing it and also come to the conclusion that my decision to follow Jesus would have worldly consequences. Worldly consequences are what caused Jesus to be crucified and His followers to have to endure some of the things that He did. At this time, I found out that Philosophy is a class that challenges your faith to your face.

Poem: The mask has to come off.

They say as a Christian, we have one important mission—

To win souls for the kingdom before we close our eyes.

I agree, but we tend to let down those battling issues tucked within and broken on the inside.

You see, Jesus sat with the sinners day in and day out, but us as Christians we pout and shout at the ones whose lives reflect the ugly words coming from our mouth.

Lies told, hearts souled to the darkness and madness.. sadness caress the eyes of those who feel that life is tragic.

Where's the magic or physician who healed the sick?

He's not a genie but one who picked.

12 disciples our modern society would have rejected.

Reminds me of the drug addicts, porn stars and alcoholics neglected.

We as the church have failed to prove that the True and Living God exists.

We are so caught up in the soap operas we missed... as the drama unfolds I wonder do we know,

That God is displeased with the actions of those who know the Gospel.

The Good news that salvation is free to the poor in spirit and often the meek.

We are weak.... gossiping, showing bitterness, and then can't shake the bondage underneath.

The sheets of the smiles we put on our faces, when the inside of the mask shows tears wasted.

Let's face it. We have work to do because Jesus didn't die for us to play games,

Our ultimate purpose is to bring Satan to shame; we gave him the name of every person we are connected to... one thing holds true..

We are losing the battle, not putting our pride aside; I'll be damned if the truth became a lie.

Wake up, you who are sleeping, take the mask off; souls are weeping.

Eyes display sorrow with reality; they look at Christians like our walk is a fallacy.

See me, I agree, we have done some damage.

We have shown a perfection that doesn't exist, missed the mark of the high calling,

In hell, angels have fallen... Christians will we be next?

God is not pleased... let's hear His request.

Sure, we all have some troubles, but I doubt that God can't give us double. We have one mission and one mission only,

To hear, "Well done my Good and Faithful servant, your walk with Me was worth it."

So, Christians, take a stand for Christ, walk upright, hold tight and become the light.

Poem: The mask has to come off.

That shines when it's pouring rain, so that atheists, Muslims and Hindus can know His name.

What a shame it would be to chase money and fame to end this life casting blame.

On the one who knew no sin; told us to follow Him and die within.

No, this walk is not easy; it requires sacrifice and God-pleasing.

To study and show thyself approved, to stand out from the among the crowd not be smoothed.

To be the Bible and Testimony of the Resurrection.

Be a reflection of Matthew, Mark and Luke... Pull in Brother Paul and Peter too.

Their lives impacted the world as we know it; we need some more Elijahs, Isaiahs and Jeremiahs not fools.

Where are the Queen Esthers and Ruths? The Lydias and Marys who didn't play it cool.

Maybe some Pastors, Teachers to live out their truth, carrying on the legacy of Jesus, I'm rooting for you.

Moses, Jacob, Abraham as well; they were warriors not engrossed in a shell.

Un-Afraid to step out into the unknown, they knew that God's Spirit was following along.

Be brave Christians. We only have one mission. Take off the mask and Give God the Glory,

Let His Love Story portray itself with all its Gory.

Be proud of the fact that Christ chose you. Now Choose Him and Gain Eternal Life; Change the narrative and Win the Fight.

Going back to the movie, *The Passion of the Christ*, Jesus begins preaching the gospel as a young boy. For Jesus to start His ministry by the age of 12, this proved so many of those wrong who have stated that God can't use children or young adults to preach His gospel. After years of going to the Temple to preach the correct way of Life, Jesus finally goes to meet John the Baptist, in which He is Baptized. The Scriptures have told us consistently that baptism is required for you to fully receive the Holy Spirit in the way you need to. It's not just a must, but it's a requirement as a follower because you are following in Jesus' footsteps (Jesus was baptized. Hence, we have to do the same!!!!). Once Jesus was baptized, the gates of heaven opened for Him to receive recognition from God that He was well pleased. As Jesus' journey continues, He encounters many of those who have "religious spirits." Those people who followed the teachings of the Old Testament were known as the Pharisees and the Sadducees (expanded on earlier information). Since Jesus performed wondrous miracles on Sabbath days that challenged the religious perspective of God from the Old Testament, He was oftentimes engaged in heated discussions with them and shut them down because it disrespected His authority. They would see the signs and miracles He would perform and hear the words being spoken, and still, it was not enough for them to acknowledge that He was indeed the Son of the living God and speaking the truth that was necessary to set the people free.

I explain this because oftentimes, we ask God for signs and miracles, not realizing that He does it right in front of our eyes. I had to come to terms with this, and I still, to this day while writing, am learning what God can and will do. Jesus challenging their doctrine prompted retaliation towards Him, consisting of their desire for Him to be crucified before the celebration of Passover. Jesus knew all of their plans, and He also knew that it had to happen in order to fulfill the Scriptures and for Jesus to take the sins of the world onto the cross. As they plotted, Jesus continued to spread the message about God's love and the eternity that awaits those who will and will not choose Him.

Jesus, choosing to show the world that God always wins by defeating death, proved that there is no obstacle or no problem too hard for God and also that we are more than conquerors despite what the world says.

Jesus being led to Calvary is an extraordinary visual of how rough the walk will be for us who choose the narrow road and also to be able to look our enemies in the eyes while reaching our destiny. Before Calvary, there were feasts and parties held because of Palm Sunday. Palm Sunday is the week before Jesus' crucifixion, where the crowds placed palm branches in the path of Jesus on His way to Jerusalem. As Jesus rode along, He received a vision of those same people in the crowds a few days later screaming, "Crucify Him." During this time, Jesus and His 12 disciples had what is known today as the Last Supper. The last supper was so significant because firstly, Jesus foretold them that one of them would betray Him and secondly because it would be the last time that Jesus sat and ate with them in the flesh. He also told His disciple Peter, who told Jesus he would never leave Him, that he would deny Him three times. As He passed the broken bread around for each to take, He told them this bread is for my Body. After each had taken a piece, He passed around the wine in symbolization for His Blood. After explaining to them that one would betray Him, the dinner ended. Jesus felt so heavy because He knew what was to come. He left with three of the disciples for a moment to go and pray. Jesus prayed three times, asking God to take this heavy burden off of His shoulders. This is when He states, "Father, let Your will be done." Jesus let God know that although this burden is very heavy, if it is what He (God) wanted Him to do, then it HAS to be accomplished.

> Life Change: Imagine working at a job, having a relationship, going to school, and trying your best to become successful. You have all these plans, and then one day, someone walks up to you and asks you, "Have you given your life to Jesus?" Now, you, as a person who once failed to believe, become curious as to who this stranger that came up to you is speaking of. They ask

you to step aside for a moment and then begin to explain to you as a prophet who God is and His only Son that we have been given for the redemption of our sins. The person then goes on to explain to you what happens when you submit yourself to Christ and how the re-born process goes. You become so intrigued by what the person states that you have no idea that Jesus is dwelling inside of that person, ready to receive you as His disciple. The person then goes on to tell you that something recently happened to you that the stranger shouldn't even know about. Now that they have felt your pain and introduced you to Christ; it's time for you to decide whether or not you're ready to accept Jesus as your personal Savior. While in tears, you can't believe it because this is exactly what you needed. You give your life to Christ that day, and for the next few weeks to months, God transforms you. You had all these plans and things going on for you, and then your relationship thrives with Jesus, and He tells you to let go of all of your plans and follow Him. You're scared because, one: you're not sure it's Him that speaks, and two: you have no idea what to expect if you let all these things go.

This is the time of some tests and trials. God will test your faith in Him by asking you to let go of the people who will hinder your process, but you may hesitate because they mean so much to you. Everything you have worked so hard to accomplish is now about to come crumbling down. Do you continue to follow Jesus and let God's will be done, or do you run away and forget your calling because the burden is too heavy to bear?

Jesus knew the road ahead was about to be torture and very painful, but He knew it had to be done. Imagine if Jesus decided not to obey God. How much worse would the world be, and how much of God's wrath on everyone, including His chosen? This would've been way too much to endure. God knew that in order to keep His people from sinning, He had to send Jesus to take the keys of death and hell away from Satan, conquer and become victorious for those who choose Him. While Jesus knew the time had come for His betrayal, He walks back after seeing them asleep three times, and after the 3rd time, He states, "rest now for the Son of Man is betrayed."

Judas, the betrayer, gave the people a sign saying, *"whomever I shall kiss, the same is he: hold him fast."* Judas came forth and said, *"Hail Master,"* and kissed Jesus. After witnessing Judas' betrayal, Jesus watched as one of His disciples cut off the ear of one of the priests and had to let him know that it was enough and healed the man's ear. *"He who lives by the sword shall die by the sword,"* (Matthew 26:52). They took Him away. From there, Jesus is mocked, whipped and tortured because He loves us and knew that God's will had to be done. As He walked to Calvary, Jesus was beaten, kicked, punched and everything in between.

At times Jesus stumbled and fell, but He continued on His journey. At one point, Simon was given the command to help Jesus carry the cross. I lift this information from the Bible and movie for this lesson; as we journey the narrow road to heaven, we meet people who God has destined to cross our path so that we can minister to them and help them find their way to Jesus also. Simon helping Jesus on the cross was Jesus showing us how He would help us carry ours. Though Simon told the crowd that Jesus' blood was not on his hands, Jesus is willing to take the blood off of our hands and clean them.

The representation of the walk was how we are to be Christ-like. Not that we will be nailed to a cross (unless God decides), but that, through the walk, we will be called names, beaten down by the world, tortured, spit on, and humiliated for living out our faith. On earth, we have a mission to complete for God in which the only way to do so is by giving our lives to Christ. Once you have surrendered to Jesus and the Holy Spirit inside of you, the doorway is now open for communication through Him to the Father. The only way this can happen is if a person is willing to submit to God and receive His instruction on what to do and how to do it. After being nailed to the cross, Jesus is raised and lives eternally in the rest of God. This reveals that despite what we endure in our flesh, if we choose to follow God, our spirit will forever be in His rest and the victory is eternal LIFE.

God proclaimed in Genesis that we were created in His image. I don't know about you, but being created through God's hands and in His image is just amazing and even greater knowing that He intended your greatness for His glory. Not only is this great for acknowledging your worth and your calling in God, but it also takes heavy understanding and wisdom to reflect on exactly what God means when you're called to become a prophet or whatever He has gifted you with to be used for the intention of helping rescue souls that need salvation. Opening the Bible opens the door to the mind, heart, and, most importantly, the Spirit so that He can fill you up and then help you to comprehend it for your own understanding, to be used to discern when working in ministry if it's from the Holy Spirit or demonic spirit because the enemy also knows the Scriptures.

The reason why it's so vital to know that the enemy knows the Scriptures is because he can use them and twist them into making a believer misinterpret what God has said. Using the gift that is placed inside must be thoroughly strengthened and cared for, so the recipient doesn't get confused. I personally had moments where I had to learn when God was speaking to me because I would hear different voices. Not to say I'm mentally ill or anything of such, but this is what happens once you open the door of your ears so you can receive instruction. My mom has also told me that once you have opened that Bible, prepare to be attacked, and boy was she correct; but, I will explain more as the story unfolds.

Once you learn how to read and interpret the Bible (I have come to know that this takes time), we are now able to properly reiterate the Word in order to publicize the anointing and use it for God's will.

Poem: The mask has to come off.

Before God makes His will come to pass, the person must first be birthed through the parents that God chooses.

God revealed Himself to me in a new way that I didn't experience the first time I went up to the altar. In this time of surrendering my life, I understood God a lot more and knew that because I had just been given an opportunity to make a turning point, I could never turn back to the chains that held me in bondage. I have learned through my journey that God is remarkable and amazing. He took what man would call trash and turned it into treasure. In the world, I was considered to be unworthy of Love or Forgiveness. My great-grandmother always told me about God whenever I would visit her. She knew before I did that God loved me more than I could ever imagine.

Prayer

ABBA!

Thank You for dying on the cross for humanity's sins. We have no idea the pain You went through just to call us Your own. I pray this prayer for the one who doesn't know the sacrifice You made for them. The world is pleasing to the eye, but its fantasies are deadly. You came to earth to give us life and life abundantly. What a tragedy that some choose to render that gift, the gift that leads to eternal life. Many play with the idea that at the end of their life, everything is over. I pray that instead, they would see the purpose and meaning behind their existence. The material things in this life can't compare to the wonder and awe of heaven. For non-believers and believers alike, You are to be revered as the true Master. I pray that this chapter would reveal all that You have done and the expectation set before humankind as they acknowledge You are real. The Bible is not a fairytale or ancient legend; it is to be cherished as words that echo Your Love for us. I plead the blood of Jesus over each person who comes in contact with this book, especially this chapter that gives understanding of the work on the cross. Father, this glory is not for me, but through You, it brings hope. May You be glorified, honored and praised, Amen.

Mr. Right?

College was a trying time in my life. I was still trying to recover from the emotional and mental abuse I encountered at the hands of my foster mother. I had no intention of seeking to meet someone as a partner. I had just gotten a job at Marshalls in Elmont, NY. I remember applying for the Home Depot that was next door. I interviewed with one of the managers, who told me that I would be required to start work at 7:00am on a daily basis. My responsibilities would include helping them load and unload trucks to put out supplies. I knew that by the end of our conversation, I wouldn't be taking that job. I was a college student who enjoyed taking classes in the morning because I was used to it. The freedom that came from having morning classes and the rest of the day off was music to my ears. Now that I wouldn't be able to take this job, I needed an alternative.

I remember seeing the Marshalls next door before I went to the interview. I made a mental note that if this didn't work out, I could just swing by and see if they were hiring. I previously worked at a Marshalls in Freeport, NY, when I lived in Roosevelt. I went over after the interview and asked to speak with a manager. I explained that I once worked at the Marshalls in Freeport and wanted to know if they were hiring. She told me that they were. I completed the application and went about my day. The operations manager called me a day or two later, stating that they would be starting a group interview session and that I was invited. I went to the interview and was offered the job on the spot. On September 25, 2013, I was officially an employee of Marshalls in Elmont, NY. Working at Marshalls was the usual. I was a cashier and knew how to do the layaway department; at least that was a lie I told. Due to me "knowing layaway," I began working in the department when they needed someone.

I began to work with this guy. I call this guy, Randy. Randy was the store "hottie." I say "hottie" because honestly, he was and still is very attractive. He was one who could have any girl because he had the height, skin tone and smooth voice. We began to interact with one another because we worked in the same department. About a few weeks into working at the store, I noticed that Randy was catching my attention. This was more noticeable during a particular time in the break room. I was going in there to grab something in order to go back up front and work. Randy was already in the break room. As I walked in, I could feel his eyes staring at me. At first, I shrugged it off because I really didn't care, but as I started to walk back to the door, I paused; his eyes were on me again. I asked him his name and then walked out after he told me. I didn't pay any attention to it at first because I was new to the job and really didn't have any interest in dating, or so I thought.

Things began to change as I was out with my college roommate and her boyfriend. We had been invited to see a live performance in Manhattan. My roommate and I had gotten free tickets from her boyfriend because he was one of the people who lived on campus and could give tickets to college students. When we arrived, the line was out the door and around the corner. My roommate's boyfriend gassed us up by telling us we were VIP for this event, but that plan fell apart because so many people showed up. We ended up turning around and heading back to campus. At this point, I know some of you are wondering what this story has to do with Randy. Well, I'm getting there.

We headed back to campus. It was a chilly night in October. Each of us now had to replenish our metro cards because the train was coming. We all hopped on the train. It was packed as usual; the city never sleeps. As we got past the areas where most people would get off the train, I found a seat. As I pondered what just happened from the concert, I felt a pair of eyes staring at me. I looked over and saw Randy with two other girls. I said hello to Randy and was met with a snare from one of the girls he was with. I again paid no attention to it. The following day at work, Randy asked the cashier point person if he could have the register next to mine. We spoke as customers came to our registers. When he noticed that no one was on the line, he asked me what I was doing in the city at the time that he saw me. I explained what happened at the concert and all. I asked the same, and he mentioned that the night I saw him was for his birthday. He told me that I should hang out with him and his friends sometimes. I agreed, and then we exchanged Instagram names. Over the next few days, Randy and I would be stationed next to one another at the registers, just talking. There were two days when I didn't come to work. When I returned, he explained that he had called up to the job looking for me, but I wasn't there. I later confirmed that this had actually occurred from another co-worker.

Over time, I began to like Randy. He was attractive and showed some type of interest in me. I was in awe. I recently had fallen out with a "potential," so to try and move on, he was able to grab my attention. I began to tell the foster sister I was living with at the time about Randy. She told me I should tell him about my feelings towards him. At first, my shyness kicked in because I had never told a guy how I felt about him. I was used to guys coming up to me or asking me out on dates. I decided to push past my comfort zone and do what my foster sister suggested. I texted him and told him that I liked him and wanted to get to know him better. I didn't receive a response for two days. While on the bus, Randy had finally texted me back. He stated that he wasn't ready for a relationship because he wanted to get back with his ex. He believed she was the one that he was going to marry. I was stunned at his words but didn't know how to process them. I'm not sure if I responded to that, but I know from that conversation on, I went on a roller coaster ride with Randy.

By that time, it was evident to Randy that I was into him. Though feelings of rejection plagued my mind, I kept pushing through, believing that he would change his mind. I mean, why show interest in a woman if you are thinking of someone else, or, for that matter, woo her with no intention of starting a relationship? Randy was starting to act differently. He wasn't malicious or anything, but now he had me at his fingertips with this new revelation. Each day we would work together and flirt with one another. During this time, I was still getting high, so my mind wasn't in the right place to really understand the concept of friends with benefits and being "strung" along. I admired the fact that Randy was very persistent in talking to me but not really showing interest in going deeper into whatever he wanted to call it. I figured he just needed time; I was looking dumber and dumber. He would show interest in me in person through our conversation, but over the phone, mostly through texting, he was distant and disconnected. I would always have to text him first, call when he said call, or chase him. Some days I didn't even get a response. I was truly infatuated with this man and didn't care that he was stringing me along and playing mind games.

Eventually, as our co-worker/friendship progressed, we started having more conversations outside of work. One day, two other co-workers (Jay and R) and I, along with Randy, went to McDonald's and got some Italian ices. On our way back to work, I showed Jay my phone because of a post I thought was funny. In the background, Randy was playing the song by Sean Paul, "When you gon give it up to me." My other co-workers thought the song selection was funny, but I didn't pay attention to it. We finally pulled back up to the job and got out. A few moments later, once inside, I realized that I didn't get my phone back. I went up to both Randy and Jay to ask them if they had my phone. Both of them denied it. I searched frantically for my phone. Randy assured me that he would go back through the car and look to see if I had dropped it.

I decided to purchase another phone and counted the one as a loss. I messaged Randy to see what he would say. He wrote me on Facebook messenger to tell me that someone had texted him from my phone. I sarcastically responded, "that was me." To be quite honest, I was checking to see if he was the one who had taken my phone. He told me that he had checked again for my phone in the car but didn't find it. He assumed that Jay had stolen it because he was the last person I gave it to. Realistically, I don't think anyone stole it. I may have dropped it while getting out of the van. That one incident pushed us to talk more.

The following day I met a friend of Randy who used to work at Marshalls. When Randy picked her up, he didn't know how to introduce me, so I said, "Hey, my name is Tanisha." Randy looked relieved because he didn't have to justify who I was to him and spare my feelings as well as keep what he was thinking inside. We went to a pizza restaurant just to hang out and get some fresh air. When I sat down, Randy sat next to me, and this new friend sat in front of him. I got a sense of her feeling really awkward being around the both of us. I wasn't sure why I had gotten that vibe, but she, like many other females I encountered throughout my time of knowing Randy, would show the same thing. I later learned that they had sexual relations. Randy was a playboy.

We finished up at the pizza place and then headed back to Marshalls. Over the next weeks into months, I was attached to Randy's hip. He didn't need to communicate with me every single day. He didn't respond to my text messages often, but in person, it seemed as though things were going well. Randy never expressed that he wanted a relationship with me. He did, however, make sure that I knew he wanted to have sex with me. He would always make sexual jokes towards me. I would often feed into it, and then nothing would happen. Things changed one day when a co-worker whom I considered a close friend had a conversation with Randy. She shared something personal that I had told her with him. With this information, his sexual conquest intensified, but I didn't give in. I had made a vow that I would wait until marriage to have sex.

He began to change before my eyes. I no longer could see the guy that I really liked in the beginning. He had a mission instead, and that mission was to get me to his bedroom. It became a game to him. He would say inappropriate things like, "I'm an expert with my tongue," reference sexual posts from Instagram and talk about blowjobs. Over time, my frustration towards him intensified because of the fact that our conversations would be centered around sex any time we were together. We were in one year of friendship, and things hadn't yet changed. He was very distant when it came to communication. I was stalking him on social media to find out if any girls liked his pictures. I would look at comments and literally lower myself before him just so that he could continue to take an interest in me.

In 2014, his direction totally shifted. He stated that he was applying to another job and that he wanted to better his life. He had taken the test to become a civil worker and passed it. He would now be working for the state. His hours at our job changed. I started to see him less and less. Eventually, he only came to work once a week. During this time, each day that he decided to work, he would drop me off at home. Once he had this new job, the communication grew even worse. I wouldn't hear from him for days at a time. Again, I was the one reaching out to him. Even though he may not have responded, I doubled and even tripled the text: no response. I look back now with disbelief that I allowed someone to entrap me "worshipping" the ground they walked on.

Eventually, he began coming back to work for one day out of the week. According to Randy, the reason why he came every Tuesday of the week was to spend time with me. He would work each Tuesday and then drop me off at home. The conversations were very shallow and usually involved him expressing his sexual frustrations with me. I became his target which brought on his desire to conquer the conquest. I would be the one to satisfy his sexual frustrations. While aware of the newfound revelation, due to lack of maturity and a strong male role model, I continued entertaining him. It became a cat and mouse game for both of us. He was chasing my body, and I was chasing his heart; neither of us won the game. It grew to the point that one day while dropping me off at home, we saw a man running out of his house to the car in a firefighter uniform. He said to me, "What if his wife was giving him a blowjob?" Fed up, I asked him why was it that he always chose to talk about sex with me. His reaction displayed shock. His response was, "I'm a Scorpio." He began to feel uneasy. I mean, I had been feeling uneasy about it every time it was brought up, so it was such a great feeling knowing that it's finally registering that he needed to stop.

He dropped me off in silence. I begged him for a hug before he pulled off. He knew that physical touch was my love language, and getting a hug from him made my night. Belittling myself, I often had to beg him for a hug. He would sometimes want to hug me before I went inside, but they were side hugs, ones that didn't feel genuine. I didn't quite understand how much energy I was investing in this man.

For the next few months, our conversations seemed to become drier. There had been a shift in our lives. He was clearly upset that I asked him that question the night we were in the car. He would still make sexual hints. At one point, before pulling off from the store, he put his hand on my thigh, and I moved my leg to signify that it wasn't going to happen. Outside of the fact that the car conversations weren't going so well, he still wouldn't respond to my text messages. I was falling even harder for him because I thought it was the "gentleman" thing to do by taking a woman home. He became much more disconnected in person; he would continue to show interest when he saw me talking to other men, and other females at the job took notice of this, as his actions were obvious to the outside eye. He made sure that he intervened when he saw me engage in just a hint of flirtation or friendly conversation with another guy: jealousy, I call it. It bothered me that he couldn't or wouldn't say he wanted a relationship but tried to control any guy I would make reveal the least bit of attraction. It was interesting; he didn't "want me" per se, but no other man could have me. SMH! Co-workers would make facetious comments about it. One of the girls said to me as he came into the store for work that she thought it was just me that liked him and that he had no interest in me because I didn't look like his "type." I was able to put the pieces together and understand how she thought I was chasing after Randy. Little did she know though, I was. I didn't show it publicly as much because people are nosy, and honestly, we weren't in a relationship.

Since my co-worker stated this, it had me thinking that Randy actually liked me. She wasn't the only one. During another instance, I guess I hadn't answered his text because I wanted him to know what it felt like to not respond to someone who cared about him. I walked up to the register, and he asked me where I was while another young lady was observing. I answered, "I was at work and school." We didn't say anything after, but I could see from the look in his eyes that he was fed up with me not giving him attention. I so desperately wanted him to feel all the pain he was causing, which triggered from his ignoring my text messages, not calling me, and lack of communication skills; but, one thing for certain, he knew that he wanted sex.

After that incident, Randy became more controlling. Whenever I didn't respond to his text messages, in anger, he would emphatically question me as to why I didn't respond to his texts. I mustered up the strength to tell him that this is what it felt like when he didn't respond to me. I started playing this new game with him in which I was determined to make him "feel" how I felt by how he was treating me. I eagerly wanted him to wear the pain I took on. I should have caught on to this before, but my constant infatuation with him, as well as smoking on a regular basis, got in the way. I couldn't see Randy for who he was, but deep down in my gut, something wasn't sitting well with my spirit.

The year 2015 came through, and that's when things really took a turn. One of my co-workers began carpooling with Randy, unbeknownst to me. I found out one day when he told me that he was giving me a ride home, along with this girl and a male co-worker. He told me that I was to sit in the back because he was dropping the other girl off last. I felt embarrassed because I was being forced to sit in the back while this other female co-worker was getting all of his attention. That situation didn't last long because a day or so later, while we had just finished our shift, we began to clean up so that we could all go home. I saw Randy and the female who now had his attention, having a conversation across the aisle. He shook his head no to something and then walked away. I made my way over to the girl and asked her if she would be getting a ride home tonight. She said, "no," and then asked me if I was getting a ride from him. I responded to her that I wasn't sure.

What occurred next really shocked me; she stated, "I know he's going to give you a ride, Tanisha," and then walked away with her head hanging low. I was stunned. I figured he was losing interest in me, and for her to say that meant one thing in my mind: he had used her for what he needed and refocused his attention on me. The same girl, for weeks, would have her head down whenever I walked by. It was like she was ashamed of something. He mentioned a few days later that there was a rumor going around that he had sex with someone and told me, "It wasn't true." I fell for it, although I never heard that supposed rumor.

The disappearing act from work picked up again. He would miss weeks. I didn't understand why but I was feeling really neglected at the time. He returned just as I was about to give up to the fact that maybe it was time to move on. I often wondered from a man's perspective if it's an ego-booster for a man if a woman tells him she's interested and he has no intentions of taking things to the next level. We walked into the operations manager's office to put in time off for various reasons. He explained that he had been missing in action because of the new job that had just started. He bragged about the fact that he would now be making $14 an hour. On the inside, I was jealous but didn't let it show. How come with all that he was doing to me, he gets to make a decent living outside of this place we called a job? I knew that after our conversation, we weren't going to see each other anymore.

One of our last conversations took place in May of 2015. At that time, I stopped texting him as much. I was slowly awakening to the fact that I was dealing with a woman collector: a man who puts a woman on the shelf and, when he wants to, takes her off and plays games with her heart and emotions. I was too naive to see the lines of jars called woman stuck on this shelf waiting for it to be "my turn." This reminded me of the saying, "As long as a man knows you are emotionally available and he's a boy trapped inside of a man's body, he will always return."

I really became distant to the point that I resorted to online dating websites to meet other men. I found some interest in 1 or 2 of the men from the websites, but Randy still had a hold on my heart. I believed in my heart that he was going to be the man that I would marry. Blinded by the enemy, I couldn't see that when he told me he wanted someone else, he meant it. I was dreaming of him on a daily basis. He consumed my everyday thoughts. I was a feign as some would call me. I became obsessed with Randy. I fantasied about what it would actually be like to have sex with him. The destructive thought pattern continued as I would often masturbate, just thinking as if he would be the one who would please me even more. I didn't fully comprehend that this toxic situation was taking a toll on my relationships with friends and family. I figured that Randy was all that I needed. I always thought he was having the same feelings, although in person, it wasn't showing.

Being consumed with a man who wasn't really my man put a dampen on my spirit. Between the dreams of seeing him with a wedding ring to dreams of having children with him, I was sold on the fact that he would eventually change into the man of my dreams and come to the reality that I was his one and only. As the month of May continued, God began to deal with my heart in different areas. I could feel the tugging, but I was pushing back because God was getting in the way of this relationship I had with Randy. I put God on the side, thinking that he would "catch up" to the fact that this was going to be the person I married, and God needed to get with the program.

As the light began to shine on the fact of who Randy really was, a chain of events happened that pushed us further away from each other. I mentioned the story of the Hotbox at the beginning of the book. This would be the first and last time I ever smoked weed with Randy. I was thrilled at the fact one of my co-workers I smoked with regularly asked Randy if he wanted to smoke with us. He looked at me and then said, "yes." I contained my excitement, but I held tightly to the thought that we would finally be on the same page and that smoking together would draw us closer to one another. We had all planned to meet up after work like usual. My friends' and I would all find our way to a remote spot away from an area where we wouldn't get caught. We would call the weed man, and then the hotboxing began. Tonight was going to be special because Randy would be a part of the crowd. We all got into different cars, but Randy and I rode with some of the crew to the spot. We were showing each other posts from Instagram and just having a grand time before stopping. I couldn't believe my eyes. I was awestruck at the fact, the experience that I only dreamed of was getting ready to happen.

    The blunts had been rolled, and we all passed them around. Blunt after blunt, we kicked it and laughed. It felt like a movie scene: the girl with her favorite guy and all the friends just enjoying each other's company while the "couple" are mesmerized by each other. My experience soon came to a closing end because God had plans for me that night. As we continued to pass around, my high took a turn. I started feeling like my spirit man was leaving my body. Like an out-of-body experience, I thought I was going to die. I began to cough uncontrollably while my body was being split into two. I couldn't handle the box, and one of my guy friends noticed. He said, "You good, Tanisha?" I told him yea, but it just kept getting worse. One of our other guy friends that were in the car told me to step out because it seemed like I couldn't handle the box. When he said the box, he meant that I couldn't handle how much smoke was inside of the car. I stepped out and went behind the tree, hoping that Randy would get out of the car and rescue me. I was in for a rude awakening because he nor any of the other guys in the car stepped out to assist. I secretly cried out to God to help me out of this situation. I looked up at the sky, but God didn't pop out and speak to me. My high just slowly abated, and I was able to get back into the car. Randy asked me if I was okay. I explained that I was fine, but deep down inside, the embarrassment could have easily just shown up on my face. I was annoyed and horrified at the fact that no one got out of the car to check up on me. I guess being befuddled and out of the right frame of mind really didn't help it to register to them that someone was in distress.

We finished smoking and then all headed to the gas station/corner store. I didn't get out of the car, but I was in the front seat of the car. Randy asked me again if I was okay, and my response was the same. I looked back at him to see that he was extremely high, and his mind was so clouded that anything I experienced just a moment ago had already gone out of the window.

We finally got back to the spot where we smoked. Randy asked if I was ready to go, and we were on our way. I was used to being able to focus just a tad bit because I had done the hotbox many times. We got into his car and just sat for about five minutes. I told him that it was okay for him to pull off, but he didn't understand. For the next 10 minutes, we sat in silence. Randy finally broke the silence and asked was I ready to go. I sarcastically replied, "I said that 20 minutes ago." Still trying to come down from his high, he started to drive. The awkward silence continued until he wanted to stop and get food. I responded by saying I didn't like to eat after smoking. He was very persistent to the point that I thought he was going to take me home and it would be over.

On the way home to where I lived, Randy decided that me saying no to eating was a lie. He pulled closer to a chicken spot and said that we were going to get dinner and then head back to his house. I knew I had to think of something fast; the high I was in made processing slower, so I repeated that I didn't want to eat. He pulled into the chicken spot even as I obliged. To him, smoking with me was the key to getting me to finally have sex with him. Once we pulled into the chicken spot, he turned the car off and prepared to get out. A number of big men begin to fill into the chicken spot. Randy seemed to be scared of this thought and wanted to wait until the men left. After about two minutes, more men went in; Randy got even more nervous and shut down the idea of getting chicken from this area. As we were backing out, he said we were just going to head to his house. I panicked because I knew what that meant. Either I was going to give in to him when we got there, or I was going to be raped because I kept saying no.

As nervousness settled in, Jesus stepped in. As we were at a red light, a vision flashed in front of us both. God had shown us the direction to get to the house I was living in. I knew Randy had gotten the same memo because he got nervous and just said, "I think I should take you home." The look of relief couldn't have been more evident. I told him that I agreed, and he headed in the direction to take me home.

He dropped me off, and we didn't talk to each other for a few days. The night of me having that out-of-body experience led me back towards God. The few weeks after were a blur, but now it was at the end of May. I started going to church again. I had met some other students from my current church there. They told me about it, and then I figured I had nothing to lose by attending services. One Sunday, I listened as the preacher began to call people to come to the altar. I could feel the tugging of God, but I didn't move. The ministering got even stronger. God sent conviction to my heart, and she walked up to me. She said, "Today is the day." My salvation was there, and God had opened the door for me to surrender to Him. I released my hands into the air and surrendered to my Heavenly Father. A series of events happened that allowed me to know that God was ready for me to take on His will and follow Him.

I was sure that things would be just like the last time I let go. This time was different. My life began to change. I was still head over heels for Randy, but God was pulling me away from him. Work seemed different as well. I still struggled with smoking weed; somehow, my friends noticed, and one in particular, randomly out the blue, told me I could smoke weed and read the Bible but that I shouldn't smoke the Bible pages. I took heed to it, not understanding the spiritual realm. Things with Randy shifted even more. I started talking to him about God more. It definitely turned him off. He looked at me with utter disgust as if what I was saying was regurgitated vomit. Talking about sex seemed to bring conviction to him; just giving that up seemed like a chore. At work, he seemed annoyed by my presence. I would talk with another co-worker who was a fellow believer about this newfound revelation of God. She would have some insight about who God was and how she had been baptized. While we were talking, I explained that now I would be waiting for marriage to have sex. I wanted to do this before I was saved, but now that I had encountered God, I wanted to do whatever was necessary to please Him. Randy overheard our conversation, then walked past me and said, "We should have sex before marriage." I wasn't shocked, but I was, however, frustrated because he seemed determined to make that happen. I, of course, ignored him, but as usual, I entertained Randy and his foolishness.

Following my conversion, the attacks from the enemy began. I knew that my time with Randy was coming to a close, but I was determined to save him. On May 23, 2015, I had a really bad stomachache while at work. I was throwing up and had diarrhea. My body felt weak, and I knew I wouldn't make it through the rest of my shift. I asked a co-worker who I considered a friend at the time to take me to the emergency room. As she was driving there, I could hear God clear as day telling me that I was going into a "Job Season." I didn't quite fully understand what God was talking about; however, I was getting ready to get the program because things had gotten serious. I ended up in the hospital for three days. At this time, I wondered if Randy was going to contact me and if he even cared about the fact that I was in the hospital.

The time had come and gone from being in the hospital, and I had yet to hear from Randy. Following my release, I got home and was very angry at him for not knowing what had happened to me or tried to find out. I later realized that I should have told him I was in the hospital, but honestly, that wouldn't have made a difference. The next day after my release, I decided to take a walk to get fresh air. On my way out, Randy had finally texted me. He asked if I was at work. I was so angry at this time that I didn't respond to his text message. Instead, I went ahead with my walk. I was finally cleared to go back to work. I was ready to face Randy and explain my frustration with him. The day never came. Once I got back, I learned that Randy put in a two weeks' notice and would not be returning to Marshalls. I never got the closure I was seeking. I got home, opened my Bible, and then broke down and cried. The anguish of releasing the pain I felt because God had just removed him was overwhelming. I cried for a solid 10 minutes or so. The tears on the pages of Genesis reminded me that I was on the path to a new beginning.

From 2015 to the middle of 2017, I didn't see or speak to Randy. The last text message that he had sent went unanswered. During this time, God really shook me to the core. He was breaking off things I didn't fully realize were holding me back from embracing all that He had for me. Though hurt by the fact that I had given Randy so much of myself, I wanted to reconnect with him so badly. The torture in my mind from missing him, yet being angry at the same time, took a toll on my emotional state. As I tried to process what took place, God began to ask me to pray for Randy. Pray for Randy? I was thinking, "You can't be serious, God." Well, God was certainly serious, and I certainly needed to obey Him. I struggled with this for a while, pondering why I would pray for such a person. The heart tug was consistent to the point where God had woken me up one morning and told me to pray for Randy. I replied out loud, "No." I went back to sleep, but when I awakened, I couldn't get up for the life of me. I felt as though God had just smacked me upside the head, not because of Randy, but I had just told God "No" like I was somebody. I learned a valuable lesson that day, and it took for me to get knocked upside the head to realize it. I finally mustered up the will to pray for Randy. God revealed that the prayer wasn't for him but for me to start extending forgiveness. To take this deeper, at a small group I started to attend at my church, the leader asked us to ask God for a specific person He wanted us to pray for, for at least 10 days. By then, God had told me Randy before she could even finish talking.

The next 10 days had me excited—this time for what God was asking me to do. I prayed and prayed for Randy. God was doing a heart check on me throughout the process. I was finally starting to understand forgiveness. Afterwards, I wrote a letter to him expressing how I felt and that I believed God was going to reconnect us someday. In the letter, I had in my mind the thought that he would again be the man I would marry one day after God had saved him.

In April of 2017, I reconnected with an old co-worker from Marshalls. We had hung out together with Randy a few times, and with our reunification, I knew there was a possibility that I could see Randy again. Before we crossed paths again, this co-worker had dropped a bombshell that Randy had been in a terrible car accident. He explained that Randy's car was totaled due to being hit by a 16-wheeler. With this news, part of me wanted to jump for joy because I figured he had gotten some of his karma back, but God was still healing me from what happened, and at that moment, God made it clear about praying for him even more. Randy had been placed out of work because he couldn't walk. This ordeal lasted for six months. That night after hearing the news, I got down on my knees and prayed that the Lord would allow him to walk better than before and to draw him closer. I wasn't sure if I would ever see the answer to my prayer. I just trusted that if it was God's will that we see each other again, it would happen.

At the time, I began hanging out with this co-worker again, and I was dealing with my own issues. I knew that seeing Randy would be a sacrifice for the moment. I was currently in a shelter that required me to be back at a certain time. The co-worker and I shared the same birthday month, and he called Randy in order to hang out for his birthday. In my mind, I gathered the thought that maybe this would be the day that I finally get to see him. The fellas made plans to meet up at a certain time of the night. I was so ready to have this face to face after not seeing him for almost two years.

The time came for us to go and pick up Randy. I sat in the front seat of the car until we were in front of his house. As he locked the door, I moved myself to the back seat. I figured the guys would want to be upfront and just chat while we were on our way to the next destination. Randy took a look at me as he entered the car. I sat silently until he said, "how are you?" I asked him if he was talking to our friend, and he said emphatically, "I'm talking to both of y'all." I told him I was doing good. He didn't seem interested in talking to my co-worker. Instead, he continued to ask me questions. It had been a while since we last talked, and I never responded to his text message. Deep down inside, both of us were really happy to see one another. He asked me if I had graduated college and if I still worked at the job. I was happy to let him know that I definitely graduated college and that I was no longer working at Marshalls. He was shocked about the Marshalls thing, but I could sense some insincerity about the fact that I had graduated college. He asked me what I was doing since I wasn't employed at the place we met; "a teacher," I told him. He jerked his head around behind and smiled, saying, "You're teaching people's bad a** kids." I chuckled and responded, "I am." We awkwardly waited in silence after that. Then, I mentioned to my co-worker that there was a possibility that I would be moving back to New Orleans. I wanted to know if he'd be down to help me move some of my stuff. In total transparency, I wanted Randy to hear that this could be the last time we would ever see or talk to each other. I lied, telling my co-worker that I needed to head back home because it was getting late. He told me that he would drop me off at the train station as soon as he picked up another person. We got to the train station faster than I expected. Once there, I exited out of the car. Before I could leave, Randy turned to me and asked me why I was leaving. I couldn't really give him a solid answer, so I told him that I just needed to be home at a certain time for this night, that he should enjoy the company of his friends.

I walked inside the station with a big smile on my face. I finally got to see him and speak again. To make it better, he was walking as if the accident had never occurred. Over the next several days, I thought about him and the encounter we had in the car. I wanted to talk more about the fact that my life had changed for the better and explain the changes that had occurred in his life. The time had come for me to actually move back to New Orleans. Mentioning it to Randy and my co-worker in the car wasn't enough for me. I reached out to Randy via Facebook Messenger to let him know that the move was taking place, and I wanted us to hang out before I left. He asked me for my phone number. The Facebook messaging turned into text messages again. He told me that he had asked for my number from the co-worker, but he never gave it to him. He wanted to know how I was doing and what had been going on in my life. We chatted for about an hour before ending the conversation for the night. The feelings came back again. The hope of us actually being together flooded my mind. We talked to each other via phone calls and text messages over the next 2-3 days. We made plans to hang out outside of the plans to do this with our other friend/co-worker.

In May of 2017, the day arrived when I would hang out with Randy. He had already let me know that he would be taking me out for dinner. We arrived at the restaurant. I made sure to get a fresh pedicure and new sunglasses to spark up the attention. An old friend had just given me a sundress to wear for my birthday. I knew it would be perfect to wear in front of Randy.

Here I was dressed exquisitely from head to toe, going out on a date with Randy after almost two years. We texted each other throughout the day before getting dinner. We were both going to be late for dinner, but I honestly just loved the idea of us spending this time together. Once we made eye contact, he hugged me for a good one minute before letting go; he took a look at me and then hugged me again. The hugs reassured me that he truly missed me. We sat for dinner and just talked again about what new things had occurred. I told him about a situation that happened at Marshalls and my excitement to start a career in teaching. Explaining why I was moving to New Orleans came up in conversation, and then we moved on from that. Dinner was great! He paid for our food, and then we headed outside for fresh air.

For some reason, it felt like we were starting over. I knew in my heart it was going to be a waste of time because I didn't know if, after that day, we would see each other again. Getting fresh air was necessary. We didn't talk much outside. It made sense because our time was up. He asked me when I was coming back to New York; I knew, but God wanted me to withhold that information from him. Instead, I told him I wasn't sure. I had peace throughout this entire time. Some things had changed about him; but, overall, he was the same Randy I had encountered from Marshalls in 2013.

We said our goodbyes, and May of 2017 was the last time I saw Randy. We did speak a few more times after I moved to New Orleans, but nothing consistent. God had officially closed the door. At times I still struggle with the thought that God would save him, and we would reconnect again. God reminds me that Randy wasn't the man He designed for me. I have accepted the fact that the one He has for me will not emotionally oppress me like I experienced with Randy. One of the positive aspects of this was finding my worth and God giving me a poem to express this for any other woman who may be dealing with this type of reality.

Poem: You are Worth the Wait

You laid there bare naked and soul exposed as you had just given him your all.

The linger of his cologne still on your skin as he redresses and heads out the door, you begin to think if you should run after him, although in your gut, the answer is no.

He doesn't turn back.... realization sets in that he only wanted relations, not a relationship.

As the betrayal hits, you scream in anguish because you fell into temptation after making several vows to God that you would wait until marriage.

With your head hanging low, you pick up the pieces of your heart, hoping that instead of feeling shame and guilt, you can release the filth.

You feel confused, hopeless, angry that you allow him to trap his lies, his disguise and ultimately his demise in your mind, body and spirit once more.

You're sore from the movement and rhythm to a beat that's not yours.

He scored.... one down, many to go.

A game that he has played all so well, is it well with the heart that he has shattered?

You thought cooking for him mattered, you thought buying him gifts mattered but did you know that he had more than one batter of cake that opened the door for him to take all that he wanted.

You questioned your worth and felt as if the jewels of your crown were just buried in dirt.

He captured you in the realm of shining teeth and eyes that made you feel weak at the sneak peek of the tool in the middle of his pants.

He pants and so do you, he fooled you and then promised a ring as soon as the release of his semen inside of your treasure ended at the climax.

His lust is taxed to the max, he freely gives to any woman who is clueless about her identity in the Father.

He looks to see the voids you're lacking and wants a chance to add to the pain.

This ain't sunshine, just rain. You believe that if you remain faithful to a faithless foe, he would change.

Sermons of changing a man doesn't connect that only God can fix a man. Sunday after Sunday, you run to his arms, as Satan does more harm using this man to destroy what has just been planted.

Granted, he tells you he's a Christian, he displays fiction, but every week he likes to make friction and defy your restrictions of waiting to the day when God says yes.

He says undress and lay on his sheets, then your souls meet time and time again. At the end, he says, I'm just your friend.

The ring of the phone could have kept you from falling, but you figured it's just a little thing.

Your worth has been snatched because you have been giving it to Satan's seed, trying to fill a need that can only be filled by the King.

Knowing a tie that binds can't be unwind, you search for any dignity seeping through.....

When the sting of rejection finally became apparent, the tears started running down your face like your eyes had been sprayed with mace.

It burns.... your soul, your heart and slowly, you begin to learn that the only Heart you should yearn for is God's.

My Sister

—∽—

Dry your eyes, for in due time, God will send one of His men whose spirit exudes the God within so that you don't have to pretend that you're in Love but can thoroughly enjoy the Master's Plan and Win for the First Time in Your Life.

The man He has doesn't want any strife, he is imperfectly made in the Perfect Image of the True and Living God.

Trust that the Father knows exactly who you need, so freeze on looking for the reflection of darkness, and Trust that a knight in shining armor doesn't exist but one who Loves God you won't be able to resist.

He'll respect your boundaries, lead to the altar and give you stars no falter.

The purity of his heart won't be fake because he knows that God's Wrath is at Stake, and he doesn't want to displease the Master.

He'll be patient in a world that says move faster.

He will guide you being led by the Spirit, trusting that God will provide y'alls every need. He won't feed into the foolishness of the world because he knows that the world was conquered during the Savior's appointed time.

His Love won't cost a dime or nickel or penny for that matter. You won't catch him out drinking Henny, waiting for the next Jenny or chasing the next cake batter.

His love will grow fatter for you over the years, and like ears, his soul will be pierced to treat you with such fierce intensity.

He'll be sensitive to your gentleness, won't rush and taint something that time will reveal.

He'll know that you're his one and only, not play games because he's lonely.

So trust in the one who knows no sin, to introduce you to his best, the Love will stand against any test.

So rest in the Match Maker's Palms, Re-read the Psalms and Worship at the Altar.

One day you will turn around and see the man God has for you doing the same, then God will move you to shake his hand, and y'all will exchange names.

What lesson did I learn from crossing paths with Randy?

Having daddy issues and not seeing a Christ-like relationship between a man and woman, may have been one of the reasons why I fell into this trap. I lacked a void that could only be filled by God. Sure, I had seen marriages in my family, but as I got older, my eyes were open to the reality that these were indeed very toxic. God's Word is true when it tells us to train up a child in the way they should go (Proverbs 22:6). As parents (whether current or future), it is an obligation to show healthy relationships. Children watch our every move. Training can either be for the better or the worse. I had only known toxic relationships as a child, so as an adult, it seemed very familiar. As painful as it was watching my mom and grandmother experience such tragedies, I couldn't see the red flags that flashed when I met Randy.

The headlights to the car allow you to see ahead before you get to a certain point on the road; God showed me from the moment he didn't respond to my text message about my feelings towards him. At times, I blame myself for the mishaps that occurred, but I'm very thankful to have gone through a season of this. It has given me the much-needed perspective on watching out for red flags, as well as knowing my place as a woman. Oftentimes, we hear of women taking control and telling a man how she feels about him without direction from God. We tend to take matters into our own hands, thinking that a man will be turned on by our chase. Understanding the roles between a man and woman from a biblical perspective is a necessity. At the moment of his rejection, that should have been my cue to walk away and leave things where they were.

I was desperate, and my desperation was revealed because I continued to pursue Randy. From constantly knowing that his agenda with me was to get into his bedroom and then tossing me to the side, my clouded judgment and lack of self-worth gave me a promise that didn't exist. This is to us whether male or female. When someone makes it clear that they are not interested in a relationship with you (emphasis is you!), take that heed as God's warning. We have become so accustomed in our society to make someone love us when the one who does is Jesus. I remember this quote, "we accept the love we think we deserve." When you don't know or understand the love of Christ, it is so easy to allow someone to take you for granted despite authentic love. The heart is deceitful above all things, and society tells us more often than not to follow our heart.

Now don't get me wrong, God does give us the desires of our heart. The issue is that people tend to take this Scripture out of context. Some Christians tend to take the pieces of God's Pie (Bible) to fit into how we want it. The Scripture (Psalm 37:4) clearly states, *"Delight yourself in the Lord and He will give you the desires of your heart."* We must first surrender to Jesus, giving all things to Him. This Scripture also corresponds to Matthew 6:33 and the 1st Commandment to put no other 'gods' before the true living God. Randy was on a pedestal that I placed him on. In so many ways, I worshipped the ground he walked on. I was determined to be his 'Lord and Savior,' although twisted, he was mine. As mentioned before, Randy consumed my every being/thought. When God removed him from my life and unveiled the blindness in my eyes, I finally understood that my daddy issues could only be fixed by God. It was settling at least to say I have a 'man.' He, like my biological father, was in and out of my life. Having no purpose or intention of bringing me closer to the Lord, he left me in broken pieces. I had to seek God and get God's will for my life. The void has been filled by my Heavenly Father, and I'm now fully aware of my worth. I trust that one day, God will introduce me to His best, and I will know that this man will be able to lead and pursue me. I won't be confused about whether or not he wants a relationship. This man will make clear that he heard from God concerning me as his wife, and he has God's permission to pursue. He will be the type that doesn't have time to play games because he is ready for commitment. With a personal relationship with Christ, he's the guy that knows if he breaks my heart, he is breaking the heart of God because I'm His daughter.

I trust that God's best will be a strong communicator, allowing me to know that he's not here to waste my time. He will plan dates and actually make them happen. A man who can keep his word and not make lame excuses as to why he didn't do this or that. I have yet to encounter such a man. I'm tired of boys trapped in men's bodies with no idea who they are. I have the assignment as a woman and wife/mother to be in submission to the Lord. My husband will be in submission to the Lord as well. This will allow us to display a true relationship with God. I will not have to pursue him in any fashion; he will know that I'm his wife before God reveals it to me. That is such a sobering feeling.

As the poem says, he will be imperfect, but one thing will hold true; God will be evident in his life (fruitful), and he will know that I'm his one and only. We have to hold on to this truth. God is still in the business of bringing kingdom marriages/relationships to the forefront. And one other thing, marry your Best Friend, get to know one another before getting into a relationship. Know what makes each other sad, angry and happy. Be content in knowing that if he/she is for you, a friendship can lead to such a thing. Rushing into something headfirst always brings a concussion; test the waters and make sure that they value the same things you do. Most importantly, they **MUST** have their own relationship with Jesus. Unequally yoked relationships bring a lot of heartaches; I'm telling you from experience and discussions with other friends. God knows exactly what He is doing. Love Y'all.

Although the poem didn't really relate to my situation with Randy directly, having the knowledge that somewhere in this world, a woman is unaware of her worth. Your story may not look like mine;

nevertheless, knowing your worth is so much more important. I learned a valuable lesson by trusting in God to introduce me to one who loves Him deeply. No time is too far or distant too long; anticipation of waiting for a man who knows that his identity in Christ will match yours. You are worth the wait, my sister/brother. God knows us better than we do.

Prayer

Heavenly Father!

    What a chapter! Love is misconstrued in today's society. We have so many versions of love except the one that is indeed very true. Today, I pray for the heart that has been broken by someone they believed was the definition of true love. The enemy has blinded us to think You don't know the real definition of love and that You are not to be trusted; what a lie from hell. I pray for words of wisdom and encouragement to come to the person who idolizes someone else with hope that they can fill the voids in their life. For the person reading this prayer, I pray that they would come to know You for the understanding of what love is. Lead them to peace that enables them to love You first and then themselves. Thank you, Lord, for this beautiful soul. I pray that they will forever know how deeply You love them. In Your Name I pray, Amen.

The Prodigal's Daughter ✔

The story of the prodigal son is very familiar to those of us who have read the Bible ourselves or attended church services. It is one that compels us by the Holy Spirit to run back to the Father after we have made a mistake because His arms are wide open. The prodigal son believed he had it all figured out. He asked his father for the inheritance that he knew would be there for him when he was ready. Somehow, the son believed he knew that the time was at hand. The father allowed the son to take his portion and do with it as he pleased. Immaturely, the son wasted his money for momentary pleasure. He came to a complete low, realizing that all his earnings had gone. The pride in him said to work and earn money for fear of shame going back home. Eventually, humility got the best of him.

The son recognized that his return to his father was the only hope. With trembling and fear of the unknown, the son walked up to his father's estate. The father, because of the love he had for his son, saw him from afar and, being overflowed with joy, ran to his son. The return of his son back to the father displayed the love God has for His children. He knows our shortcomings and has already given us the solution. Fear has a tendency to force us to humble ourselves before the throne and utter with lowliness, allowing conviction to settle in. One may think that God will somehow punish us for our sins when it is His grace that beckons us to submit. Thankful that Jesus has already taken that penalty, it's liberating to know that our story doesn't have to end. I'm sure that the prodigal son realized this the moment he saw his father running to him with open arms. I have fallen short of the Glory of God.

For years, I struggled in my relationship with God because I didn't have good earthly relationships with Christian people. The church I was attending at the time didn't really invest the time to help me become a real disciple. On one hand, I attribute my lack of discipleship to them because discipleship falls in alignment with what the Church is called to; on the flip side, I could have made a stronger effort to take the initiative of developing my personal connection with God. The lackadaisical support level provided by some churches after introducing babes in Christ to the Holy Spirit amazes me. Failure creeps in because we forget that newborn Christians need a support system to get them to the place spiritually that God intended. I don't believe you can work out the salvation of another person, but it is crucial that they feel the love and support from the body of Christ. Struggling to understand that God wanted me to know Him for myself came with the fact that I was rebuked for opening up a Bible or praying in the house of my old foster mother. In her home, she was god.

Coming to terms with the fact that she was god in the home, didn't really register in my mind until God allowed me to leave. I faced more personal attacks from the enemy through her because I had no idea that spiritual warfare existed nor the fact that diligent Bible study and prayer was the key to understanding the tactics of the enemy. She knew that I started going to church almost every Sunday to get away from her. I guess the enemy in her didn't like it. She would say sly things to me, most I don't recall.

One particular instance, I do, however, remember was me talking to her about something that I was bothered by. She bragged about all of her accomplishments. She had a fancy home, nice cars, and a host of lavishness. The words echoed from her lips, "I'm like god" —the audacity. Baffled by this statement, I went downstairs to the room I was sleeping in. I don't even remember what she spoke after, but the fact that she compared herself to the true and living God was mind-blowing. That situation catapulted me into the next phase of my life. Things began to change as I came to terms with how she was treating me emotionally and mentally. The abuse was enough to understand that I needed to get away from her.

During this season in my life, unable to really develop a personal relationship with God, it caused me to be that prodigal child. No one at church gave me a blueprint to follow God, so it was more compelling to go my own way and keep God in the background. As I progressed into going to college, the enemy had a plan. I promised myself that I would never smoke weed because I knew the implications were very toxic. Somehow still, my freshman year allowed me to experiment with the new drug and led to an addiction, amongst other things. Smoking was therapeutic. It allowed me to escape the reality that I finally got away from my old foster mother. Though I used it to drown out my sorrows, the opposite effect took place. I spiraled out of control. The addictions of settling into the darkness pushed the Holy Spirit out of touch in my physical life.

Although I had these moments of pain coming to me non-stop, not having a genuine spiritual walk as my current reality didn't stop God from pursuing me. While in my freshman year, I did talk a lot about God in a religious aspect without fully comprehending who He truly is. As explained before, freshman year was spiritual attack central. However, while living on campus with an old friend in my sophomore year, we would talk about God often and have moments of worship. I felt connected and disconnected with God. Somehow in the back of my mind, I knew that God was real, but coming face to face with this darkened heart of mind wasn't at the forefront. I was still smoking (with my roommate as well), struggling with pornography, and completely lost in the world.

In 2015, after the episode that occurred from the hotbox, God began to draw me back to Himself. I was lost but still believed in God. Over the next few weeks, my life began to change. The misfortunate event that happened with Randy pushed me in the direction I needed to go. I was still attending St. John's at this time; I was a junior. I started going to a worship dance group's practices on campus. I had made some friends in the group, so it was usual that I went to most events that they hosted on campus. I grew close with some of them over time and, at one point, was a part of the dance ministry.

While this was happening on campus, I decided to return to Perfecting Faith Church because it was where my first encounter with God occurred. I prayed to the Lord to allow me to see one of the women who helped shape my walk with the Lord. I went to the church with my co-worker, who would hang out with Randy and I often. We got to the service just in time. I looked around to see if I would see her, and God allowed me to see that she was there. I was going to make it my mission to see her before I left the church for the day. After service was over, I called out her name as I walked up to her; she was overjoyed, and so was I. I couldn't believe that God had answered my prayer. We talked about how it had been some time since we last saw each other. Just seeing her was so freeing; she was a real woman of God. Ironically, that day we saw each other, she told me she had prayed that God would allow her to see me again. We walked with my co-worker to the front. My co-worker told us that he was going to hail a cab for us to get back to the train station.

Once he went outside, she and I began to chat about what God had been doing in our lives. As she started to share her testimony with me, God did something beautiful. I was standing in front of her by the door. We were about 6ft away from it. I needed to continue looking out for my co-worker because any minute, the cab could have come. Focusing my attention back to her, we continued our conversation when the door blew open. It was the most peaceful wind I have ever experienced. We were both shocked but not surprised; it felt like God had blown us both a kiss. I interpreted that was God answering both of our prayers and letting us know that He heard us and was pleased with the request. We chatted some more about the experience we just had and went our separate ways. That day was the beginning of all the ways God would reveal Himself to me. I didn't know what He had in store but getting that kiss from Him was enough for me to continue to surrender so that I could have more encounters with Him.

The encounter I experienced with the Lord at St. Johns was the boost I needed to keep going. God was doing miraculous wonders in me. I was still going to the dance ministry's events. I didn't continue dancing with the group for personal reasons, but I did perform a testimony solo on stage at one of the shows. I began having intense dreams during this time as well. God was showing Himself to be true in my life. I was still smoking but not as much. Around my birthday, the dance ministry scheduled a lock-in. The lock-in was a night of worship, spoken word performances, and the fresh Word. We danced and sang our way through. I began to see into the spiritual realm, and God revealed some demonic things that were happening in the atmosphere of the lock-in.

Before it ended, we were split into groups to discuss different questions pertaining to topics that Christians faced in their walk. I met a few girls and a guy that I had never seen prior to this event. When the session was over, I chatted with the guy and one of the girls for a few. He stated that he attended a church that wasn't too far away from us and that I should visit. He told me the name, and I assured him that he would see me there one Sunday. A group of us from the dance ministry decided we should go visit the church. I didn't go with them that time; I went another time on my own.

I stepped into Church of the Harvest for the first time on my own. I recognize some of the people from the lock-in. I chose to sit apart from the dance ministry for personal reasons. I enjoyed the service and was approached by one of the girls in my group during the lock-in session. She asked if she could pray with me. I remember part of the prayer was for God to have a hedge of protection over me as I go through my test. She said that the test was to prune and strengthen me. I wasn't sure what she was talking about, but I knew that I would be coming back to this church because it had such a profound impact on me from the time I stepped in.

The following Sunday changed my life. After the preaching of the Word, it was time for the altar call. I was hesitant at first because I had gone up there before, and nothing had changed; God had other plans. The minister came next to me as the music was playing and touched my shoulder. She said, "Today is the day." I instantly felt a prick in my heart and a desire to surrender to God. Over the next few weeks into the months, God began to remove people from my life who were no good and started the process of sanctification. I was still smoking weed at this time; an old friend had told me I could smoke and still read the Bible. I believed in this lie. The panic attacks resurfaced, not as strong, but God was making a point.

One night, I tried to see if I could smoke and read the Word. I opened the Bible after I had just finished smoking. I realized I couldn't get through it, so I shut it closed. Opening up social media was the next option. I opened up Instagram, and as I scrolled, I came across a picture that showed Jesus standing over someone while drawing them out of the water. I instantly felt in my spirit that God wanted me to become baptized. Getting baptized was something I looked forward to. On Facebook, I viewed posts from a guy who kept sharing different Scriptures on following Jesus and dealing with relationships. I decided to follow his page and check him out. He talked about how his church did baptisms each week and that if anyone wanted to, they could just reach out to him and let him know. I knew that God had called me to this part of my life, so I reached out and asked when the baptism would take place. He told me when I could come and to be ready.

In October of 2016, I was baptized to publicly symbolize the acceptance of Jesus as my Lord and Savior. It was quite the experience; I left my past in the water. The freedom I encountered as I emerged out of the water has stayed with me forever. I didn't know what to expect with this new life, but I put my trust in God that He was going to take care of my needs. I remembered as I read the Word that after being baptized that Jesus went into a season of testing. I believe that every Christian, after being baptized, will experience a season of testing to begin the process of sanctification.

That same day I witnessed another guy being baptized. We hugged each other because to us, it was like God was shining His light upon us. As we walked to the train station, we talked about the freedom we felt after coming out of the water. I began to share with both men that God had blown His Spirit on me before I was baptized and that He has shown me an outline of His face in the sky. After the baptism, my encounters with Him became more frequent as well. I would see visions of Jesus on the throne while I was praying; this one has always stuck with me specifically because the throne room was huge, and He would show me sitting at His feet. I looked like a little girl dressed in all white. Another time, He took me into the spiritual realm and allowed me to see that He was answering my prayer as I prayed. Sometimes I could see His Spirit sitting in the room with me while I read the Word and prayed.

Having these intimate moments with Jesus rendered my soul so much comfort. To know that I went from struggling to reading the Bible as a young woman to now being in a full-blown relationship with Christ was mind-blowing. I made it my mission to spend time with Him as much as I could. I was living with my mom again because of circumstances that had come from living on campus due to the foster agency. God began to deal with me about some of my pain that came from the hands of my mother. Praying for people who had hurt me seemed tedious. At times, it was easier to make that happen, but for others, I just couldn't muster up the strength. It was frustrating some days to read the Word and pray. My gift of discernment had come in full force since being baptized and I became aware of spirits trying to disguise themselves as people in my life. Though I was struggling in some parts, one particular person who helped me understand God much better was my great-grandmother.

Since I returned to New Orleans on different occasions, I made sure that when I was down there, I would visit my great-grandmother.

She loved some Jesus, Y'all! Her relationship with Jesus was so evident. I felt constant peace whenever I would visit her. She was a breath of fresh air. I could freely talk about Jesus with no judgment, and she would always have a story to tell me. I looked forward to times when I could visit her on my own. I remember that after I was baptized, she was the first person I called.

"Grandma, I got baptized." Her heart was overjoyed. She congratulated me and told me how proud she was. We talked about God but knew we couldn't stay on the phone for too long because then we would be talking for hours about the Lord, and I needed to get home. I assured her that we would continue when I saw her again. A few months came and went. I started attending Church of the Harvest every Sunday. It fed my soul. Pastor Curt preached in a way that made sense. He articulated the Bible and made it clear that we had to have our own personal relationship with God in order to grow spiritually. I had found the peace I was looking for. Each Sunday, I looked forward to church. There were many young adults there who were my age, and many of them helped me see how important and valuable I was to the kingdom. They would invite me to hang out with them and pushed me to strengthen my relationship with God. Outside of constantly having a great-grandmother who was praying for me, having these new friends brought joy. Though I know God to be real and that life was seemingly blissful. It didn't stop the spiritual warfare lurking in the shadows.

I reached a place of maturity in my Christian walk and realized that it came with many personal attacks. The enemy was furious because I would no longer allow myself to be a broken soul in his kingdom; I belonged to Jesus. I knew that I had some soul-ties that needed to be broken. God finally allowed me to discern how dishonest Satan really was. I was heavily into witchcraft. I practiced following horoscopes, read tarot cards, and watched and listened to ungodly content.

One day while reading my horoscope, as I did many times, I gathered that my lover was going to call me. I waited the entire day only to witness this not come to pass; I was deceived. This was the first of the schemes revealed to me that the enemy uses to deceive us. It didn't register at first because I was at the babe stage of my Christian walk. Now that I had become more aware, I wanted to be free from it all. Finding ways to combat the enemy sure had its challenges. Prior to this, I had no knowledge that there was a war for the souls of human beings. Having no knowledge that spiritual warfare was the reason why many were blinded, I came face to face with the real deal. Before I became baptized, I figured I could wage war with Satan using physical tactics. I didn't realize the power darkness possessed because I was in darkness myself.

With the veil torn from eyes, no amount of my own works, per se, could prepare me for one of the weirdest nights of my life. As I slept, I awakened to something that startled me out of my sleep. I turned to a particular direction because I could sense something in the room with me. I turned to see a really dark figure a few feet away from me covered in what looked like something Darth Vader wore standing near me, holding on to a pitchfork. As dark as it was in the room, this figure was much darker. I could feel the presence of God so strongly covering my entire body. Fear tried to creep in, but the Holy Spirit prompted me to go back to sleep as it was already being taken care of. I obeyed and slept so peacefully. It was the most peaceful sleep I had in a very long time.

I woke up the next morning to the same smell still permeating the room. It was so close to me, like it had left my body but was looking for an opportunity to possess me again. Eventually, the spirit left the house.

I called my great-grandmother to speak with her and say Happy Birthday. My great-grandma and I had a birthday one day apart. We always made sure to call one another for our birthdays. Reverting back to our conversation, she was talking to me about what she was going to do that day. As the conversation continued, her tone changed, and it was like she was no longer talking to me. She was saying, "I know who you are." I asked her if she was saying something to me, and she assured me that she wasn't. Before ending the phone call, she said to be mindful of the enemy because he will use those close to me to try and discourage me or mock God. I thanked her for the warning, and we hung up.

I could smell that entity still close by. It was starting to become more annoying because I wanted it to disappear and get away from me. I decided to go and cook dinner to get my mind off of things. While in the kitchen, one of my brothers came in. He knocked the broom over and proceeded to try and walk away. I told him to pick it up, and he replied, "tell God to pick it up." I was shocked, but I knew that my great-grandmother had just spoken this to me. He, of course, picked it up because I didn't respond to his antics. My next younger brother came into the kitchen and did the same thing. He gave me the same response that I should tell God to pick it up. I knew from that moment it was the enemy and not my siblings trying to get a rile out of me. It was interesting that as soon as she said it, the enemy tried to get me to lose control. Now that I have gotten further in my walk, I also believe that it was God showing me that the enemy was small and didn't really have a lot of power compared to the cross. Though he tried to use my siblings to tell me what to do, when I commanded both siblings to pick up what they had caused to fall, they picked it up immediately. The next few days following, attacks from different angles began to come my way. Co-workers were saying things that they didn't before. The guy that I really liked at the time became even more distant, and I started to have many encounters with God to let me know some things and people were going to have to be removed in order for me to grow. It was the pruning season.

Another thing that happened was the mocking at work. Not all of my co-workers did this, but some of them were aware that a change had taken place. One particular co-worker told me that she could tell something was different about me. She spoke in a peaceful sense. I was able to block out the others, which was good because I didn't need to allow their words to sink in my spirit. They just looked at me with disgust because I chose to no longer engage in the same things they were doing. Some of those guys I hung out with slowly began to become fired from the job or quit.

Over the next few weeks, I saw things change on the job. I began to have more peace there, and I knew God wasn't going to have me at my job for long. One friend I made in particular, who was a Christian as well, helped me to really know that God takes care of His own. We were able to have more conversations about God because I was finally having my own walk with Him. We shared each other's struggles. She wasn't the only Christian I worked with, but we became close friends and still are to this day. While some encounters were pleasant, the one with the guy really took a 360. I wasn't talking to him as much. I was actually looking for other ways to entertain other guys. I would speak with him about God on different occasions. I could tell it was really bothering him. He tried to still have sex, but it wasn't pushy like before. He would say things like, "Stick to listening to your Gospel music" or "Follow Jesus." He wasn't genuine when he spoke, but God used him to continue to push me in the way I should go.

As painful as it was to deal with someone that I wasn't equally yoked to, my desire to please God became more important.

The pruning season God was drawing me into felt like my heart being ripped from my body, and a gaping hole remained. The pruning intensified, but my love for God grew. The negative things I experienced coming from those I considered friends couldn't compare to the freedom I found in Jesus. He began to reveal Himself more and more as I drew closer. The sermons preached by my new pastor resonated. I belonged to the Father, and no one could take me away from Him. Trials and tribulations caused me to go to dark places. Reaping the consequences of my sins really challenged this new life. I had to come face to face with my problems, and instead of running to addictions, now I had to leave it at the altar. The rude awakening that revealed itself through these trials allowed me to see myself. In all honesty, no one wants to really face oneself. The ugliness we hide behind makes it seem as though we are the better person but looks shameful compared to the Cross. The Light overshadows the darkness. God finally had me where I was supposed to be, broken, so that He could come in and shape me into His image. I couldn't even be mad at God anymore because I knew that His Word indicates that I must bear spiritual fruit. He prunes in order to produce fruit. The prodigal drew back to the Father.

Attending church became routine for me. I loved it. Experiencing the Worship and the Word, I was in my element. Although this happened to be the new normal, only one person warned me that God was going to test me, and it would be for my benefit. *Huh!! Testing me. Oh, nah, God, I'll pass.* Yet clearly, He wasn't moved by what I had to say because God needed to show me that I really loved Him. The enemy came roaring in like a lion. The next week or so after that person prayed with me to let me know God was going to test me, tests began.

In May of 2016, I got the first test as a Christian. It was nightfall, and I began reading the Word. I kept feeling it in my spirit to be delivered. I didn't understand what deliverance meant, but I knew that in order to be free from some things demonic, I needed to pray and ask God to release me from it. As I read and could feel the pressing in my spirit, I prayed that God would remove whatever was not like Him out of my life. God led me to search the internet for prayers about deliverance. I came across a website and read the information. The person on the site pasted prayers one could use for deliverance. I read them aloud and then went into what I now know as spiritual warfare. I prayed for at least an hour, asking God to deliver me from all my sins and from any spirits interfering in what He was doing with my life. I felt something break off my body. I believe it was a demonic spirit, not sure which one. After receiving peace from God and assurance that I can rest, I grabbed holy oil that my old roommate had given me in college. I put it on my hands, and then I wiped my pillows; the sheet I was sleeping on that night, and the entire sofa. I know, crazy, right? I was convinced I needed that oil to cover me, not knowing His Blood was sufficient. I anointed my head with the oil, prayed and went to sleep.

The spiritual attacks continued. While at work, my stomach began to feel like it was knotting up. I felt dizzy and had a strong urge to vomit. I got to the restroom just in time in what seemed like an eternity. The pain in my stomach was worse, and while in the restroom, one of my co-workers I call a friend at the time was there. I asked her if she could take me to the ER because my stomach was in knots. When we got to the ER, I had a high fever, and the pain I was feeling was at a seven. My co-worker noticed that my body looked really swollen. I asked her to take a picture, and I couldn't recognize myself. My body was indeed swollen. My mom came into the place where I was in the ER and the co-worker left. I thanked her and knew God had brought her there on her day off for a reason. My mom looked at me and said, "You may have a bowel obstruction." This wasn't the first time I had one, she stated, but it was years ago when I had the last one. Soon the doctors came in and said that it was indeed a small bowel obstruction, and I needed to stay in the hospital a few days until I had a bowel movement. I asked my mom to bring my Bible to the hospital and some change of clothes. I stayed in the hospital for three days. Of course, while there, I met this woman who was my roommate. We talked about the Lord, and she let me know she was going into surgery. I always believe that God places us in ways we can be a blessing to others.

Anyhow, I opened my Bible up to the story of Job because that's what God told me I was experiencing: a mini Job season. I began to understand the book better because I was in it. Not physically, but I'm sure you've heard, you never understand someone until you are in their shoes. I didn't go through what Job went through entirely, but it sure felt like it. Before I left, the woman's family had come and given me flowers and a balloon. It was such a sweet gesture, even knowing them for a small time. The woman went into surgery the day that I left, and I never saw her again.

After being discharged, I couldn't wait to get back home to the comfort of my own bed. *Whew! God, I made it.* My body went back to normal, and I received blessings following that hospital stay. Financially, God had me covered even though I wasn't at work. On top of that, the guy Randy I told y'all about, I returned back to work to find out he quit: Double Blessing. God was making it clear that I passed my test. Unfortunately, yet fortunately, Christians experience tests during different seasons. The next test sent to Heaven Gate asking God, "why am I going through this?" God didn't give me an answer, but I had faith that just like He brought me through this, He would do it again.

Prayer

Heavenly Father!

This prayer is for the new Christian. Welcome to a life of sacrifice. My prayer is that the person who God used as a vessel to draw you to Him, didn't give you a fairytale perception of who He is. This prayer is not to scare you but to bring awareness to the fact that the world's knowledge of God is false. This is the Supreme Being, I AM that I AM. This means He has no limits. He doesn't lean on your understanding to do His good work in you. Let the Lord lead and guide you in this life. It is not easy; there will be tests that make you question whether or not God is real and if He hears your prayers. God tests us to strengthen our faith. Lord, I thank You for this precious soul. I pray Your favor, grace, and mercy over their life. Teach them in the way that is true and doesn't fade. Open their eyes and heart to the spirit realm; not for fear but for the reality that Satan is after them for choosing You. I pray for peace, a renewed mind, and a fire that never extinguishes. Lord, may You be glorified, honored and praised, Amen.

Here we go again!

More blessings came after drawing closer to the Lord. It was my senior year in college. Things were starting to turn around in my life, and I was excited about the freedom I began to experience in this new season. I finally broke free from the foster agency I was under. Paying for school came through God's provision. I often wondered why God didn't allow me to have my college expenses paid for before this. Nonetheless, I can say it was a blessing not having to stress about how I was going to pay for school the next year. Here I was, getting ready to graduate college.

The life struggles couldn't compare to the fact that being a college graduate had given me access to a better future. I remember in my sophomore year as smoking weed caused my grades to decline. I dropped two classes because they were overwhelming at the time. During senior year, the mistakes I made in my freshman and sophomore year caught up with me. I had to take summer classes and struggled to figure out how to get this credit. I received advice from the senior advisor. I was able to take classes in the winter or graduate in December. I chose at that moment to graduate in December; I was disappointed in myself.

As previously stated, in May, I went to the ER because of stomach pain. This was also around the time that final exams were going on. It was my senior year of college; this couldn't possibly be happening to me, yet here I was. While in the hospital, I emailed two of my professors about the stay and was told that I could make up one of my exams and have one excused. Still hanging on to the thought of not being able to graduate on time, I went home after the hospital, trying to make a plan. On my first day back at home, miracles began to take place. Besides the fact that my professors were gracious to me due to the hospital stay, I received two refund checks and two checks from work. To top it off, I received a phone call from my senior advisor. She said, "Hey Tanisha, I have some good news to share with you. I know that you only need one credit to graduate. I'm going to bypass that credit and sign the papers for you to graduate on time." Music to my ears! Wow! God had just blown my mind.

I walked across the stage of St. John's University ecstatically with a smile on my face and victory dancing in my bones. God had seen me through. Ready to enter the next season because I wanted to put my degree to use, I sent out my resume to several companies hoping to land a job and start my career. Unsatisfied with still working in retail, I told myself that I wouldn't be still working at Marshall's by December of 2016. I was grateful to have the job but making a career in retail when I wasn't happy didn't seem to cross my mind. I always pictured how my time at a place would end or what my life would amount to. My great-grandmother used to say, "If you want to make God laugh, tell Him your plan." I had it figured out: find a new job and put in my two weeks' notice. God, on the other hand, had something else in store, like literally.

With a plan in mind to be out by December, I experienced an issue at home. Spiritual warfare manifested heavily. I began to notice that every time I opened the Word or started to pray, someone barged in the room. Ironically, no one (I mean NO ONE) came into the room any other time. Somehow, whatever they needed, it only occurred when I was spending time with God. Well, one of these days, I was fed up. I explained to my mom that it was rude to always come in when I was praying. This led to a heated argument and her telling me that I couldn't move with them when they moved. With my pride puffed up, I decided I would remove myself from the situation.

December was approaching rapidly. Determined to be hired someplace new, I began talking to customers regarding job opportunities. Desperation was at its finest. Some helped, and others shrugged. I was working in the layaway department frustrated because I was constantly overworked. Customers had no concern with the fact that their attitude and bossy ways took a toll on me. I'm often told not to allow work to stress me out, but I know that being overworked for anyone who has ever worked in retail is the "norm." One afternoon, the wear and tear of the job overtook me. Between the desire to walk out of there with no regard for finances, to frustration that God's timing was not happening fast enough, I was highly infuriated. I didn't have time to entertain the attitudes of customers because I had one of my own. I tried to mask it as much as possible, but some people just had no consideration for the fact that I was just as human as they were.

As my clock-out time approached, the department started to settle down. I was relaxing in the back when I heard a male voice drawing closer. I sighed hearing him because I needed to relax a bit and get my thoughts together while cleaning the department. The man irately came to conduct a layaway. I knew his attitude wasn't going to mesh well with mine. He didn't address me properly when I drew closer. He said, "layaway," not "hello" or "here's my slip to pick up my items." I told him that in order for me to retrieve the items, I would need to see his ID. He pulled out his ID. It was the company's policy to ask for the customer's ID if they didn't present the layaway slip we initially provided them with; and, I was in alignment with the policy. I took the ID and placed it on the computer. The guy walked away as I went to search for the bag. In the back of my mind, I was annoyed. I mean, I thought having manners or at least common courtesy was the norm; clearly, this man had neither.

I was able to find his things and headed back to the register. He wasn't there when I came back upfront, so I began to take out the items in preparation for bagging. As I started to remove them, he emerged to the department with anger. "YOU DON'T KNOW WHO THE F*** YOU'RE MESSING WITH." I was so confused. He then proceeded to say, "I snatched" his ID out of his hand. We began to go back and forth, words got louder, and he threatened to kill my family and I.

Suddenly, there was a crowd drawing in. I tried to diffuse the situation, stating that I didn't snatch his ID out of his hand. He insisted that I did. At that moment, whatever he came in with was now being taken out on me. He needed to be in control of the moment. Due to his belief that I had "taken" his ID aggressively, the power he thought was in his possession had been withdrawn. The manager on duty at the time overheard what was going on and proceeded to tell me to go to the back of the department. I said, "No, he just threatened my family, and he should be removed from the department." We had security on site, and the manager didn't bother to let them know what was going on. I stood my ground, determined not to let this fool insult me because of an assumption that I "snatched" his ID out of his hand. Eventually, I was removed and brought to the break room in order to calm down. I was taken off the register for the day and told I was placed to work in the cargo section of the store: out of sight and out of mind. Yet though I was there, the man who had come to the department never got reprimanded for what he'd done.

Dominance and control. This stranger, whom I had just crossed paths within a split second, almost took my life simply on the thought that I had wronged him. I felt powerless in the fact that I couldn't do as much as I wanted to do. How dare he come into the place where I work and feel as though he needed to take out his frustration from what happened outside of this location. Struggling to gather my emotions and thoughts, why did a man in his mind think it was okay to insult a woman? He had no regard for who I was or that I was important to someone else. In his mind, male dominion was the task to show he was in control and I dare not interfere with it even with something as small as taking an ID I needed to service him. In society, anger has done some ugly things, cause wars, division among the human race, and most certainly have placed individuals in some unwarranted situations. Catapulted into the external struggle of man vs. man who is dealing with internal issues, no person reserves to justify the right to react in anger towards another human being. At that moment, the power dynamic between a male and female came brutally face to face with a reality that left wounds on both ends. Sorrows into the reality that I allowed a man to take me out of character due to the underlying feelings of weakness masked as strength. For him, the underlying strength was indeed weakness. Two worlds collided and now there was an effect following the cause of an action. He went his way, yet I was faced with a challenge that had consequences lurking. Due to not maintaining control of my anger from hearing a threat, I succumb to the result of letting someone else control my emotions. My decision came with a price.

The following day, I was called into the office and told by that manager that I would no longer be allowed to work the cash register. In disbelief, I was so upset because I was being "punished" without an explanation. I told him working in the back was not the job I applied for, and it was something I didn't agree with. He proceeded to tell me to go home for the day. I left without another word. I had the chance to really think about what was happening at this moment. This is something people who work in retail deal with on a constant basis. It's always, "The customer is right." So many times, emotionally and mentally, it drives people to the ground because it's like you take on this slave mentality: a keep-your-mouth-shut kinda thing.

Taking the day off was what I needed anyway. After dealing with an experience, I needed time to process what happened and understand if I was justified in my approach to what occurred. I returned to work and did the floor instead of going to the cash register or the back where shipments come in. The same manager came up to me and told me I needed to sign an agreement that I would no longer work at the cash register. I told him I was not signing anything because he, as my manager, should have told the customer to leave knowing he threatened one of their employees. He told me to go back to what I was doing, and he would follow up the next day.

I wasn't anxious about the following workday. It was to be expected that he had something up his sleeve. The moment I walked in to clock-in, he told me that I needed to be in the office for a "brief" meeting. Upon entering, the store manager was in there with a look of disappointment. I sat down, and she said because I refused to sign the contract, my employment was being terminated. With the peace of God in my heart, I said okay and walked out the door. Four years of service while in college, and it took for some idiot to come in being used by Satan to push me into the next season. I was content in the fact that although it didn't look like what I had in mind when leaving Marshall's, God knew more.

I got on the first bus to the stop needed to return to the woman whose home I was staying in. While waiting for the next bus, I received a phone call from a Temp Agency that I recently had sent my resume. She asked me if I applied for a teaching position, not fully registering what she asked, I said, "Yes." She gave me a date for an interview and let me know that she'd be sending a confirmation email with everything I needed to know. I said, "Thank You," trying to contain my excitement.

Talk about God closing one door and opening another. This was the opportunity I was looking for. Though it didn't go as planned in my head, God saw it fit to make sure I would never have to work at any Marshall's store again. The time came for the interview. It didn't take long for the woman to send the email with the next steps. The process seemed very easy. I had everything necessary to begin the process of becoming a substitute teacher. I walked in the interview room, confident that I would walk out of there with a job. We were given work counselors to help with the process because they have already formulated relationships with the schools in the network. This was a different type of interview. It was like I already had the job, but they needed to know what we preferred to teach and to let us know what documents were necessary to move forward in the process. Having everything to pass the first round of it, the second part dampened my spirit. I did the background checks, the fingerprinting and medical work that would clear me to work with children. The mentor I was working with told me I needed someone to verify that I could be in front of students. This is where devastation set in. I tried going to the nursery that I worked at to get a reference, but they told me No because the manager who I was under at the time, no longer worked there. With feelings of defeat, I chose to give up on the fact that God was calling me to be a teacher.

Over the next few days, I just volunteered and tried to figure out a way for employment. At this time, I was still living with the family from my church. The woman supported my efforts to find a job and would pray with me. Though her kindness helped me to a certain extent, I wanted so badly for my life to change. I began to ask God for understanding. "Well, God, if I'm supposed to be going into this field, why the opposition?" God, of course, didn't answer, but I believe to be true that He just wanted me to trust Him.

Slowly things started to shift in the home I was living in. I was trying my best not to feel ungrateful because they had opened up their home to me. I felt like because we shared a common love for Christ, I would be very comfortable until God put me back on my feet. The change occurred about a week or so into my stay. Each morning I could hear the family awaken because I slept on the couch in the living room. The kids would stomp down the stairs, and lights would be turned on, plus calling for the kids to come downstairs to leave. This was done without regard that I was sleeping. At first, I didn't mind because, again, I wanted to be grateful that they took me in, but I began to feel like it was done purposely; I didn't have confirmation for this, but at the time, this is what I thought. Eventually, I was moved downstairs to the basement area after being given an air mattress by one of the family's friends.

Alone in the basement, I was at a low point. I had just lost my job, I was away from my family, and I began to think God had forsaken me. Still in the process of trying to get this teaching career going, I became discouraged. One of the women I considered to be a mentor had given me a call. I explained my frustrations with her concerning the job part.

She began to minister to me, encouraging me to try again and to trust that God had my best interest at heart.

After our conversation, I gained a surge of motivation in my spirit. I reflected back to my time in high school. During the summer, I was a teacher's assistant. I did this for two years. Every time I helped, the teacher gave me a card signed by the students, telling me that they were going to miss me. I kept them over the years. I love cards, and they were sentimental because words have power. One day, I searched through my collection of cards until I found hers. I was able to call the school where she worked. Keep in mind that I hadn't seen her in eight years. She answered the phone, and I began to ask for a reference to the job. She didn't remember me, but I told her that I had proof that she knew who I was. She agreed to meet me at the school. I asked my old friend for a ride to the school a day or two later. He was nice enough to take me, and I began to grasp my hope again.

The time had come to meet the teacher that I worked with previously: the one who gave me such a great opportunity to build meaningful relationships with those scholars. Feelings of nervousness would be an understatement. I entered the building and asked to speak with her. My heart was beating, but I trusted that if God had brought me to her, things would work out. We said our hellos, and she told me that she had memory loss. Another woman was with her, and I remembered her as well. I handed her one of the cards she had given me. She stated that it was indeed her signature. She then asked the woman next to her if she knew who I was. The woman replied, yes. I learned that she was related to my basketball coach, and she was around often in the high school I attended. With a yes from the woman, she said, I will give you the reference. Eight years later, it was God that opened that door again. I walked out of there with so much joy in my heart. I believed if I didn't listen to God through my mentor, I would have lost out on a great opportunity because of discouragement. I went home and prayed, thanking God for the blessing He allowed to come my way. I sent the information to the temp agency, and within a week, I was in the final stages of being eligible to work as a substitute teacher.

Considering the fact that I had a new job and I would be able to move into my own apartment. I was ready to start the journey of being an independent woman. Though I didn't have major issues with the family, it didn't feel like home. I realized that I was becoming complacent, and living in someone's basement wasn't the goal. The woman that I lived with offered me her bus/train card. She would allow me to keep the card because I needed it often; other times, she would need it back. Whenever she needed it back, she would let me know. One night I sensed that something was different, but I didn't put much thought into it. I asked her for a new MetroCard like I would do normally. She gave me one, and for some odd reason, I sensed that I should give it back at the end of the night.

As night drew closer, I returned to the house. I went into her room to say hello, and again, I could sense that I should give the card back, but she didn't say anything; so, I shrugged it off. I went back to the basement that night like normally. This night just felt different than before. I resided in the basement, so I was used to being in the dark. It was so dark to the point that I became a little fearful. I turned the nearby heater on and brought it closer for just a little light. I could sense a presence with me, but once again, the Lord gave me comfort to trust in Him. As I finally grew comfortable, I went to sleep. As I slept, the Lord gave me a dream. In the dream, I was flying in the sky. As I flew, I dipped down here and there. The dream continued, and then a huge shadow covered my entire body. I was overshadowed with a peace that I have never felt before. The shadow got stronger, and I heard the voice of God. He said, "I'm always with you, wherever you go." Matthew 28:20 confirms this for the believer.

Jesus is with us until the end of age. I don't remember the rest of it, but the comfort that God had just given me is comfort even until this day. I was awakened the next morning to a banging on the door, frustrated because it was rude, I snatched the door open, and instead of politely asking what the woman's husband needed, I looked at him in anger and slammed the door back. It was 7am. I laid back down, upset because when I'm woken up at times, it's difficult to return back to sleep.

The woman, now furious because of what just occurred, told me that when the contract we signed together came to an end, I was to leave her home out of respect for her husband. I agreed and began my day. Returning back in the evening, her husband wanted to meet with us about what had occurred that morning. Her husband still visibly upset, didn't want to reason together, and instead said he wanted me to leave that night. The woman tried to tell him differently, but I stated, "It's fine, I'm cool with leaving." With tears, I called one of my friends to tell him what happened, but he didn't answer. I moved on to call my pastor's wife about the situation. She told me that she would call me back. About 30 mins later, she called me back and said she spoke with the woman and made provisions for me to stay the night.

Shocked and in disbelief, I told her I was leaving that night and didn't care what anyone thought about it. I was so hurt because I was the one who called her, and instead of hearing what I wanted to say, she called the woman (she was a leader in the church) to get her side before calling back. In anger, I packed what I could and called a couple of shelters to inquire about available beds to sleep on. It was the first time I had ever experienced "church hurt." While it didn't exactly happen within the four walls of the building we call church, I'd just understood what happens when our sinful selves encounter one another. Broken by the fact that I trusted these people and to have this occur really hurt. I heard about "church hurt" from people who had once been a faithful member of the Christian body: stories I figured weren't justified because all are sinners and fall short of the glory of God (Romans 3:23-27). Now I was the one at the short end of the stick.

Emotions filled my heart to bitterness; and, I admit, at times, thinking about it brought feelings of unforgiveness. I believed in the Church to be a safe haven for the weary and broken-hearted. I couldn't see beyond the so-called perfection and see flawed humans needing the love of a Savior. A shock bundled into my heart, already hurting because I had already been dealing with yet another issue coming from my mom. The layers of pain soaked in like vinegar burning my healing process to the root. Maybe that's where God wanted me: completely helpless and dependent only on Him. With the imperfections of a human, I needed that situation as a reality check that only one could fill the voids lacking from all of life's troubles. I didn't hear God clearly the first time, but going through that situation amongst others surely led to an unravelling little by little.

I called shelters again to see if anything was available. I previously had done so because of an argument between my mom and me. Any outlet to be free from mental and emotional exhaustion would have helped. Due to it being late, many of them were filled already, with no vacancies. After about 3-4 tries, one shelter in Brooklyn finally answered and told me that I could make my way to their area. With just some of my things, I took the Long Island railroad to Williams Ave in Brooklyn to a women's shelter. "God, here we go again!"

Prayer

Father who art in Heaven!

You understand beyond human understanding. This prayer is for the one who is tired of going through seasons of testing, the one who is ready to throw in the towel and walk away from their faith. I pray that this would be a reminder of their prayer to prevent them from being led astray. Here they go again! Yes, again, for the belief that all trials and tribulations have a purpose. I pray for their hearts to be rededicated to Your Will for their life. Trapped in an endless cycle of war with their souls, I pray for true surrender to the one who fights all battles. Your scarred hands and feet are a true testament that You empathize with our pain. Your sacrifice is the example for each person who chooses to put all their trust in You. Jesus, hear the cries and pleas of the person reading this. Show them that You are not a God created by human hands. You have the answers to all life questions. Although we are not able to know everything, I pray for a gentle spirit to flow in this person. Heal them, Lord, and restore their hope. You give beauty for ashes. Our pains can't compare to the joy set before us. Every season is for a reason; let us not become bitter but better. For the beautiful soul reading this, I pray that they would grow in the midst of trials and trust in You to sometimes calm them and not the storm. Thank You, Lord, for all that You have done for their life already. May You be glorified, honored and praised, Amen.

4-007

My friend finally called me back as I was in the train station. He was just as frustrated as I was because we talked about me moving into the woman's home prior to me staying there. We both knew what type of person she was, but God had used her to help me before this next season. Anyway, I arrived at the shelter a little after midnight. It was strange to be in a place. White walls, silence! I felt like I was in a prison, just waiting until they called my name. At around 3am, they finally got to me and took all of my information. I was just ready to go to sleep at this point. I needed to escape the reality. I got the bed information and walked to the destination. Eerie walls, no noise, despair, and sadness loomed the hallways. I took a shower and went to the room. Beds occupied an entire area. It looked like the building used to be a school, so the beds replaced the desks. No privacy; you could hear everything that was happening in the hallway and in the room. I read the Word and went to sleep. It was 6am. I was awakened by the police officer telling us that it was time to get up and everyone had to leave the room. With one hour of sleep, I crawled out of the bed and went to the library for the day. Shelters have curfews, so I knew I only had a little bit of time to spend outside.

No job, no money, and homeless. Wow! God, is this where it has come? I honestly wasn't angry at God like in previous years when I didn't understand. I believed it to be another part of my story where God would be glorified. In shelters, they do an intake; and afterwards, you are required to speak with someone to transition into the next phase of finding housing. I got an appointment to meet with a social worker to discuss job options and the possibility of moving to a different shelter. Before going into the meeting, I was sitting out front of the office trying to wrap my head around the fact that I was here: in a shelter.

As I pondered on it, my eyes drifted to this board filled with sticky notes of those who had come to this place. Some were Scriptures. Some said things about the person. One particular sticky note caught my eye. It read, "Jesus wants to hold your hand, one scarred hand to another." Talk about perspective! That blew my mind. It was as if God was telling me that He was there, present with me in front of that office. The scars were paralyzing me to not fully understand why I always had to go through trials. From the time I was conceived up until that moment in a homeless shelter, I wanted to ask God so badly, "what is the problem?"

I couldn't question the thought that He wanted to cause pain. I remembered my great-grandmother telling me, "I used to ask God why me all the time, one day He responded, "Why not you?" The words echoed in my spirit. I admit that because I'm a child of the King, I was spoiled. I wanted the blessings of God and not the tests. It's excruciating, uncomfortable, and makes you want to throw in the towel and tell God goodbye. Welp, the moment lasted as seeing that Scripture really challenged me in this season I was about to enter. I finally had the opportunity to speak with the social worker. He told me interviews were set up for me already, and all I needed to do was go to the place where they were hiring on the spot. He began to look over my information and was shocked to see that I had a Bachelor's degree. He told me that I didn't belong in a place like that, and he wanted me out of that shelter as soon as possible. He stated that there was another shelter in Brooklyn that I could go to. He told me that it may take about three days but assured me I would not be staying at the current location. While I was waiting, I received random money from somewhere unfamiliar to me and an old friend to suffice until I could figure out what was going to happen next. God was letting me know that He's my provider. Three days later, I was on a bus to the new location. It took some time to get there because another girl needed to be dropped off, but as promised, I was on my way to somewhere new.

Turning Point. It was an interesting name for a shelter, but it was very symbolic for me. A shift in my life became apparent. I was required to fill out more paperwork, and that took some time as well. The guy who took my information finally finished and took me to the place where I would be for my time there. We walked up four flights of stairs. I was tired and annoyed because they didn't have an elevator. Wrestling with my annoyance, I finally reached the destination and entered a space that I could be at peace. As I sat on the bed and pondered on my next move, a light bulb went off.

Have you ever had a moment of an epiphany? Well, I have. 4-007 was my assigned room number. At first, I didn't recognize the connection, but eventually, I realized that this room number was representative of the date I entered foster care. To think that this came full circle eight years later signified that Turning Point was going to set the stage for my new beginning. The connection could have dampened my spirit. Instead, I actually was intrigued by the newfound revelation. What was God going to do in this season? The answer would tell itself as time went on. 4-007 was a single room. I liked the fact that I had a key to the room, and I could be alone. I honestly didn't want to have to deal with a toxic roommate situation. Between foster care and college, I had had enough. I unpacked the little that I had with me and went to sleep. This current circumstance would just have to make do.

The next morning reminded me of where I had come from. By 8am, everyone needed to be out of the shelter. In the midst of the transition into a homeless shelter, I was still in the process with the temp agency. The references came back clean, so I was able to start working. Though my circumstances said to doubt God, He made a way! Now I would have income coming in. Due to being in a shelter, I didn't have to spend much money. They provided us with food stamps and MetroCards. To some, I may have been living the "dream" because I didn't have to pay for many things, but I felt low because I just experienced a high with graduating college and being in a place where despair shouted loud. I couldn't really understand it. The shelter consisted of women ages 18-25. God used this time to strengthen my relationship with Him as well as become more humble. I had a legalistic view of God as a babe in Christ.

Life was black and white. There was no place for gray. Living amongst many who, like me, had been kicked out of their homes for a variety of reasons. A number of them were homosexual, some were trying to escape an abusive relationship, and others were rebelling against societal norms to tolerate disrespect from a parent. With the tolerating disrespect from parents, people may not agree, but truth be told, some parents really hurt their children through words and actions. Personally, I struggle with the idea of still honoring my mother because of her actions. I often question God to make sense of the Scripture. Holistically trying to heal from wounds that occur due to lack of maturity in a parent. Children shouldn't suffer the consequences of the actions from the person who decided to bring them to earth. It's not to sound bitter, but having to overcome mental, emotional and sometimes physical trauma isn't glamorous.

To think back, my mom is the root cause of a chain reaction that led to me being in the predicament I currently found myself in. Some may say, well, God brought you to it for a reason. I don't agree yet. I believe that many situations can be avoided if we have a better understanding and communicate with a child or whomever when things aren't going so well. Over the years, I have learned to see the glass for where it is; sometimes half empty, sometimes half full. We, as a people, especially Christians, need to stop being afraid to call a spade a spade. Having dealt with some of my trauma while living in a shelter, I had to come to terms with the fact that God knew I was going to be here and that He would be glorified through the circumstance. Meeting so many young women in my age group because of issues with parents opened my eyes to the reality that we get tired of dealing with the same old—talking to them and learning that some of the women's stories helped me to feel connected while I was there. Sure, there were some arguments and some fights, but when a bunch of different personalities clash, it's to be expected.

While we did have minor issues, there was laughter and joy. Most wouldn't believe that joy and laughter could be in such a place. It was like we knew the struggle and knowing that another person in the same situation or somewhat similar could ease the pain, even if for just a moment. I had no intentions of making any friends at the shelter; I figured I needed to handle my business and move forward. It's not to say that some of the women became my best friends, but it was a connection I was longing for, to be heard and seen. Though none really knew me from a hole in the wall, it didn't bother us to share stories, make jokes, and forget about the fact that we were living in a shelter where lemons were sour, and we wanted to make it sweet.

Having my own room really had its advantages, as I had time to spend with God alone. I spent time in prayer, in the Word, and going to church to fellowship, which helped strengthen my relationship with God. Honestly, maybe that's where God needed me at the moment. Broken before Him, yet joy reigned true in my heart. I had shelter, a place to eat, lay my head, and seek God for my next direction. No one came into the room when I opened my Bible. I didn't hear stomping down the stairs as I slept through the morning. Lights didn't turn on in my face. There was no shouting on a constant basis—peace in the midst of a storm. Life through Christ's started to have more meaning.

As I worked physically as a teacher, building financially through living in a shelter and developing a deeper understanding of Christ, God showed me that in this season, I only needed Him. I need God every day, but in my season of walking through the valley, it made sense for it to be just God and me. Although it may have seemed dreadful, considering the perspective of societal norms, I don't regret enduring that season of my life. God loved me during my brokenness in such a way that I hadn't fully comprehended before. He was using my testimony in the form of light to bring hope to women living in the shelter with me. I learned what true humility meant, how to love better, and, most importantly, that relationship with Him was more important than religion. Prior to being there, I viewed God in a legalistic way. In this place, He was showing me that there is not anyone who can completely look at situations with a narrow-minded perspective. I needed to let go of my old way of thinking. Self-righteousness had no place in a shelter. I was in the same predicament as those women. Their sin was no worse than mine. As a flawed human being, how could I look down upon another flawed human being? The women in the shelter needed Jesus just as much as I did.

Statistically, it was "prophesied" from the world that if I went through foster care, my life would always be in shambles. How humbling is it to know that God had His hand over me? The statistics said that if I aged out of foster care, I would be homeless, uneducated, and bound to the prison system. Yet, in the odds, I was indeed homeless at this moment, but I had graduated college, and having a criminal lifestyle was not my forte. In my case, the path created for a black woman had already been laid out but thank God for Jesus. He knew me before I knew Him, and in His tender mercy, I wouldn't become a statistic.

The drive in me to power through and make something out of the situation came through as I was riding the train back to the shelter. The advertisement discussed Teaching Fellows. While already in the education system, I didn't know that there was a way to become a full-time teacher.

I felt peace in my spirit to apply for the fellows and see where it would take me. I made it all the way to the last round and didn't make the cut. I don't have the best word to describe my feelings because I wasn't disappointed in the situation. I believed that God had a plan, and I should trust the process. When I returned to the shelter, I started going back to the drawing board to figure out what to do next. As I pondered and prayed, I kept getting an email from teaching fellows in other states. I ignored it a few times, but God drew me to it after not making the next round.

I took a leap of faith and opened the email to see what the opportunity was. The teaching fellows program had opportunities in Maryland, Indiana, and New Orleans. I clicked the link to get more information about the opportunity in New Orleans. In my mind, I knew that if accepted into the program, moving back to New Orleans would be a breeze because I had family there. The application process was easy. In the meantime, while waiting to get the results of my application, I applied for jobs in the area where most of my family lived. Within a month, I was accepted into the program and had a job interview lined up by the time I would get to New Orleans. I called my grandmother and asked her if I could stay until I had a way to get on my feet. She told me, "I have always waited for this moment. Of course, you can stay with me." I was ecstatic that God presented an opportunity for me to get experience as a classroom teacher as well as be able to leave the shelter system. *Louisiana, I'm on my way home.*

With the journey now going at a fast pace, I asked my caseworker if it was possible to get a plane ticket to New Orleans. She told me that shelters usually gave bus tickets instead of plane tickets. I had faith that God would supply the plane ticket. I went to my mom's house, where most of my belongings were, and shipped them to my grandmother's place. I ended my substitute teaching position after an incident occurred and rested for a week before my new big move. Before I left the shelter, I received news that they would buy a one-way ticket to New Orleans. To make it better, the ticket was for my favorite airline, JetBlue. I set up the interview with the school I applied to and was on my way. Oh, and let me not forget to brag on God just a little more; I got a window seat. Not sure what was in store for me next, but that new beginning feeling went through my body like electricity. I was ready to take on "The Big Easy."

Prayer

Heavenly Father!

You are the God of miracles. You never cease to amaze me. I'm in awe that You have chosen humans to reflect the image of You; that is a blessing. On earth, You know that we struggle to find peace in the midst of a storm. The grey skies that trouble us in different seasons are no match for the sunny days and shiny skies filled with rainbows. Rainbows are symbolic to the promises You made for us. They have been taken for granted and twisted by the enemy to negate what Your Word says. This prayer is for the one who has seen the victory after going through some storms. I pray that this person celebrates each victory You gave them and to be content in whatever season they are in. As brother Paul wrote, we should know how to abase and abound with little or much. I pray that they would never lose faith even when that victory may not last forever in terms of life; they can be rest assured that the biggest victory to appreciate is eternal life with the King, Jesus. I pray for their light to shine before men so You may be glorified, honored and praised. Amen.

Big Easy

Anytime you hear the word Big Easy, most will say it sounds like you're talking about the city of New Orleans. If this was your first thought, you are absolutely correct. Home sweet home! Such an interesting time in my life. NOLA is my birthplace; and, God sent me back there for a time of growth and reflection. I couldn't believe it. Never in a million years did I believe I would ever return to New Orleans. I figured since I had left so long ago, it was a part of the past that began the trauma I faced for many years. I was an adult now, which meant that my perspective on life had changed. I was no longer that little girl trying to find her way in a big area; the older version of me was curious and eager to know all that New Orleans had to offer.

Big cars, big neighborhoods, and even bigger people. I'll get to why I say bigger people in a second; but, first I have to acknowledge what I noticed after the first few months here before grasping how my spiritual walk was in for a surprise. Sin was lurking at New Orleans international airport as I landed. The pilot came over the intercom to let us know that we had landed at our destination. It wasn't until I walked off the plane and into the terminal that I could smell that New Orleans air. Yep, you read that correctly. I could smell the distinction of New Orleans from any other place I have ever visited. Clear skies cause the air to smell fresh. It was different from the air in New York. As we know, NY is polluted. Though danger lurked behind closed doors, I was ready to make a change in my life; living in a homeless shelter left me with new beginning vibes.

I called my grandmother ahead of time to ask her if I could stay in her home until I got on my feet. Like any grandma I know, that was music to her ears. She had been waiting for the day to arrive when her grandchildren would move back home. I would be the first. My grandma was waiting for me at baggage claim. She had a big smile on her face; so did I. We had waited for this moment for over eight years. The random visits to the city had shortened for some time. I came to NOLA ready to begin a full-time teaching career and to have a fresh start in life. The ride to her house was pleasant. We chatted about random things, but I could sense the joy radiating from her heart to know I would be here with her for some time. The weight on my shoulders left as soon as we entered her home. I was relieved to be freed from time restrictions, late-night fire drill alarms, and living in a temporary place with temporary people. God had done it again. I walked into the bedroom to put down my belongings. Dropping my bags and sitting down on a couch was like heaven on earth. It amazed me to think of the luxuries that come with having your own place. I miss just being able to live as a person. Though God had sustained me throughout my time in the shelter, New Orleans was home.

One thing is for sure, my grandma can throw down on some cooking; and, I, Tanisha, could throw down on a plate. For the first few weeks, that was all I did: eat good food and sit inside the house. I won't say that depression settled in like it did in Omaha, NE. However, I will say that my overindulgence is what caused my life to shift unexpectedly. Gluttony is a sin; whether or not, we as humans want to accept it. What we have in America is abused over and over again. My guilty pleasure was food. I mean, any person who I've talked about visiting New Orleans advised me that the food is really good. I can testify that it is not a lie.

New Orleans is known as the "Big Easy" because of the comfort of life; it's slow in pace. The food is so rich that it has slowly poisoned the people, specifically the black community. The food is cooked with high salt, lots of butter, and flavor our ancestors would be proud of. My intentions in mentioning this are not to turn people away from such a place as living in NOLA is such an eye-opener if you allow it to be. Already struggling with bad eating habits, moving to New Orleans enhanced the guilty pleasure of great food. The system is in overload when clogged with high fatty foods and sugary drinks. On top of eating the good cooking coming from the hands of my grandmother, I wanted to try food at every restaurant I heard was to die for (literally). I didn't own a vehicle at the time, and exercising wasn't my best friend, so everything that I ingested eventually showed up on my body. My first year there, I gained 30 lbs. I didn't even realize that my body was changing before my eyes. I was so blinded by my own self-consciousness that I couldn't catch my drastic actions in time; instead, I succumbed even more with the following year of gaining another 30 lbs. The impact of my actions became recognizable in the early year of 2019. I realized the damage of severe weight gain caused my spiritual walk to decline. I lacked the motivation to read my Bible or pray. My relationship with God spun out of control. I was still going to church every Sunday, as well as being a part of a support group, yet somehow none of that helped because I neglected to spend time with the Lord.

It is dangerous grounds to walk on when a Christian backslides. You have no idea the consequences or impact it has on your mental and physical well-being until the severity of your actions is revealed. I decided to get a personal fitness trainer and go to the gym 3-4 times a week. While it did help in several ways, my eating habits needed to be fixed, and I was not ready to give those things up. I was ashamed and embarrassed that not only did I let my body down, but I also let God down. I was so ready to take on a new life in New Orleans, and instead of celebration, I slipped into the "Big Easy" mentality.

God always has a plan when His children fall short. My prayer was always to bring me back if I ever strayed. That prayer will forever be my testimony. God heard me loud and clear because He opened the door for me to head back to NY. I recall the Lord telling me while in the shelter that I would be going to New Orleans for two years and returning because the person He had for me lived in the area. I didn't want to come back to NY because I so desperately wanted to be separated from my mom, including not living in the same state as she did. However, my mind had it made up, and God had other plans. I needed to find a new teaching position because my employer informed me that the budget cuts required my position to be removed. The two years I spent in New Orleans were up as God had told me. I tried to look for a job up until my contract ended in New Orleans with no luck. I prayed and asked the Lord to open a door in NY or in Jersey if He was indeed sending me back. I applied for two jobs with the same organization and was instantly offered an interview in New Jersey. Before leaving New Orleans, I was offered a position as a History teacher in New Jersey. I could finally say bye-bye to the Big Easy.

I knew moving back to New York would benefit me spiritually as it had done in the past. To be honest, the only struggle I feared was having to move back in with my mom. I dreaded it, but I knew God was calling me out of New Orleans; it had done its damage. I needed an awakening, and I needed it before I completely lost my way. In New Orleans, I rented an apartment and purchased a car on my own, independently, without the help of others, yet I believe it to be a lesson of its own. I wasn't ready to be on my own completely. There was still some maturing that needed to take place, and now that I have returned to NY, I understand it. Easy living, if not careful, can easily put one in a state of complacency; it happened to me. Moving back has brought the clarity I needed to realize how the Big Easy can cause damage just like Hurricane Katrina did in the year 2005. It was a big storm and took the city by surprise. Unexpected damage occurred that no one was prepared for. When I got on the flight to move down south, the storm took me by surprise, leaving some damage. I will say that I'm on the way to making all the necessary changes that will help me to continue growing spiritually and physically becoming stronger.

When I visit the city, I make sure to be more in tune with my body and not to overindulge. The lessons I learned here will carry throughout the rest of my life. Sometimes difficult seasons challenge you to think in a way you hadn't before. I hope that by reading this part of the story, you can gain the clarity to see if there is anything in your heart that God needs to expose so that it doesn't interfere with the plan He has for your life. I'm a witness to emotional eating and being blindsided; it doesn't feel good. I'm reaping what I sowed with food, but I don't allow it to hate myself any less. As a matter of fact, I'm learning to love myself more in this body I have today so that as my journey to weight loss continues, I won't make the same mistakes. God truly turns your ashes into beauty.

As God revealed I would meet His son, I'm still healing because I don't want to cut someone else with my broken pieces. I cherish this season I'm currently in to help me see myself the way Christ sees me and to be content in knowing I will be loved by someone of His choosing as my healing gets better and better. In the meantime, I'm changing my eating habits (mentality as well) and falling more in love with Tanisha, growing in my faith, writing/developing as a writer, and most importantly, living a life that's pleasing to Christ. If God so happens to send His son on the journey, I pray I'm equipped to love and support him in his journey and that we reflect the love of Christ with His church. I also look forward to sharing the testimony of when that happens in another book. The Big Easy is my past, and the Big Apple is my present. I'm thankful for where I am in my journey with God. I can't wait to share this with the world.

Prayer

Heavenly Father!

Thank You for this chapter. Some of life's lessons come in ways we don't always understand. I pray for the person who is reading this and wants to identify any addictions that may be causing them to be complacent. It is not our desire that any should wallow in sin unaware. It is the enemy's job to kill, steal, and destroy. Easy living seems pleasing to the eye but can disrupt the purpose You put forth in us. I pray that the person reading this would have eyes to see and ears to hear what You have to say. Remove the veil from their eyes and give them a clear perspective. Teach them to acknowledge You as their personal Lord and Savior, helping them to understand that by doing this, they will not be disappointed. As Your Word reveals sin, I pray for a humble heart to know the Holy Spirit does great transformation in willing souls. Your love is one no human can explain. Lord, I pray that if You have called someone to move into a different state, it wouldn't cause them to lose their faith or stray from the path You designed. Thank You for creating such a beautiful soul. May You be glorified, honored and praised, Amen.

Phew!

The book of Jonah is one many of us have heard since childhood. Even if you didn't grow up in the church, vigilance in the pursuit of your calling was taught to you. I didn't quite understand what a calling was until I had come to know Christ, but hearing the story of Jonah was fascinating. In the religious aspect of what had been done, Jonah obeyed God to a certain point. He was a prophet, one who heard God and at any given moment would give the people the Word of the Lord. Imagine being on fire for God because everything that He told you thus far soothes your spirit. That was Jonah. We would call him a modern-day street preacher. There are highs and lows in following Christ, and Jonah was going to be in for a rude awakening.

The people of Nineveh were worshipping and idolizing false gods. The first commandment tells us, "There is no other God before the I AM." Because God is a jealous God, He always gets what He wants. That is where Brother Jonah comes in. He was given the mission to tell Nineveh to repent of their sins (Gospel) and turn to the true and living God. God, in His wisdom, chose to use Jonah to deliver this message. Jonah took it upon himself to believe that God shouldn't save such a nation (*Sighs). His delayed obedience caused a storm to come aboard the ship and for him to be stuck inside the belly of a whale for three days/nights. He tried to run from the call of God, but as usual, a willing heart eventually surrenders as a sign of love to the purpose. To be inside the belly of a whale couldn't have been pleasant; it's dark, smelly, and void of human connection.

God loves people, and Jonah had to come to that understanding for three days with the knowledge that we shouldn't become a stumbling block to anyone God is trying to save. God uses the instrument of His choosing, and if it so happens to be any of us, who are we to try and forfeit it? It reminds me of Brother Paul's testimony, but that's another story for a different day. We have all been a Jonah in different aspects of life. In my case, it wasn't Nineveh that God was sending me to; rather, it was to birth a story of redemption by the Father through my pain, yet I ran from it because the idea of facing my trauma head-on was not what I wanted to do.

With all that has occurred in my life, the greatest blessing was coming to know Jesus personally. I could go on and on about my trauma, yet the healing that has taken place brings more joy. Eventually, I grew tired of running from my calling: a call to surrender to God and allow Him to use me for His Glory. I hear so many stories of people saying that they prayed to the Lord to use them as He pleased; I was one of them. How did I allow fear to override my faith when I knew the God I served has always taken care of me? It has been about 5 years since God put this book on my heart, and I'm in awe that it is finally completed. Whew! What a relief. It feels great to have done what He asked, but it cost me some lessons to learn. To any person that is a follower of Jesus, if He tells you to do something, make sure it gets done.

I've learned over the years that delayed obedience is still disobedience. There is someone or many people God is using you to reach, and wasting time wandering around being unfocused, can have consequences. Although this fact is true, I must say grace and mercy are one of a kind because, just like Jonah, here I am with the finished product: to God be the glory. The overwhelming excitement in my heart is like dancing in the rain with a smile the size of the rainbow that follows after it. I am in great anticipation, waiting to see what God does through me in this writing. One thing's for sure. This book is my first but not the last. Thank you for reading my story, and my prayer will always be that you are blessed, challenged, and in awe of what God has done in my life. Your testimony may not look like mine; however, because we share the same Father, it is glorious on its own. Step out on faith and believe in the God of the miraculous. He can and will use you to bring glory to His holy name.

Closing Prayer

—∞—

Father God in Heaven!

Thank You, Thank You and Thank You for choosing me to be Your daughter. This book belongs to You and every person that reads it. I am not the one who deserves any credit or praise for the victory that has come through. Your Spirit testified that being a follower of Christ is worth every tear, doubt and fear of failure that draws us closer to You. I pray that this writing has reflected Your kingdom and that my life is a witness of the Gospel, the story of redemption for the sins of mankind. You sacrificed Your life so that we can inherit eternal life. What a blessing! The material matters of this world can't compare to the glory that awaits us seeing You face to face. I pray that for every person who reads this book, it will push them to draw closer to You and to know how deeply Your Love stretches for them. With arms wide open, they can come to You no matter the circumstances, environments, or religious beliefs. You are the true King, the Master of all masters. There would be no new creation in Christ if You didn't draw me in with Your overwhelming love. A love so gentle and meek. I pray for any unbeliever who may read this and are confused about who You are. I'm here to tell them that they don't have to try You because the sacrifice to follow You is filled with joy. No demon or devil of any kind can stop Your Will. This is heaven's story as told by the chief of a sinner. I'm not perfect, and neither is the one reading this. The perfect one is You, who sits on the throne, ready to accept any and everyone. I love You, Jesus, and again, thank You for calling me Your own. May this book and its content bring You Glory, Honor and Praise, Amen.

www.ingramcontent.com/pod-product-compliance
Lightning Source LLC
Chambersburg PA
CBHW081306070526
44578CB00006B/816